Sermon Outlines and Illustrations

— ‖ — ‖ —

Compiled and Edited by

THEODORE W. ENGSTROM

Editor, *Christian Digest*

FIFTH EDITION

ZONDERVAN PUBLISHING HOUSE
GRAND RAPIDS, MICHIGAN

PREFACE

Preachers, teachers, Bible students and Gospel workers are always on the lookout for sermon outlines which may be the means of opening new lines of thought and study for presentation to the public. Likewise, they are anxious to secure as much illustrative material for their messages and lessons as is possible. It is with the thought of aiding such as these that the compiler of this volume has arranged the 75 outlines and 125 illustrations comprising this book. These are not meant to be used as a cane or crutch, but rather as signposts pointing the way to new fields of study and opening new vistas of thought.

For the convenience of those who may make use of this volume, the outlines have been arranged in chronological order and the illustrations are listed alphabetically by topic. Each outline and illustration is complete in itself.

The various outlines given herein have been gathered from many sources. Recognition is given to each as to its author and publisher. A large number of the illustrations have been gathered from various religious periodicals as we have used them from time to time in *The Christian Digest*.

We pray that each of these outlines and illustrations may prove useful and helpful in spreading the Gospel and that God's Name, through it all, may be glorified.

THEODORE W. ENGSTROM

OUTLINES INDEXED BY TITLES

OUTLINES INDEXED BY TEXT

INDEX OF ILLUSTRATIONS

9

Section I
SERMON OUTLINES
LOT'S CHOICE

Then Lot chose him all the plain of Jordan; and Lot journeyed east: and they separated themselves the one from the other (Genesis 13:11).

Consider the *cause*, the *course*, the *curse* of Lot's choice.

I. ITS CAUSE.

1. The chief element in determining his place in life was worldly advantage.
2. A want of generosity—selfishness; how mean to take that which was rightfully another's and that a benefactor.
3. Disregard of religious privileges. Had his heart been hot, he would not have ventured among the Sodomites; his aim may have been to convert them, but he came away without one convert.

II. ITS COURSE.

1. Downward—Earthward—
2. Gradual;—
   "lifted up his eyes—beheld" v. 10.
   "chose" v. 11.
   "dwelled . . . pitched his tent toward Sodom" v. 13.

III. ITS CURSE.

1. He lost his friend Abraham; what a friend that must have been who is called the "friend of God."
2. He lost his wealth; it was all consumed in Sodom, and he was glad to escape, even with his life.
3. He lost his influence—
   (a) with his neighbors.
   (b) with his family.

11

4. He lost the presence of God. Only two of the three who visited Abraham, came to Lot, and they wanted to tarry in the streets.

5. He lost his honor; in his drunken revelry he lay with his own daughters and became the father of the Moabites and Ammonites.

1. Behold the importance of choosing the right work, the right residence, the right companions.

2. Behold the importance of a personal knowledge of God; Lot got his religion secondhand: he went with Abraham. Abraham followed God—Lot followed Abraham.

3. Behold the best way to settle disputes—Let the other fellow have all. "Is not the whole land before thee?"

4. Behold the best way to get rich—by yielding all.

5. Behold the mercy of God—to save wayward ungodly Lot.

"PREACH THE WORD"
by
Rev. Frederick Rader
ECONOMY PRINTING CONCERN

* * * * *

"I HAVE ENOUGH"

Esau said, I have enough. Jacob said, I have enough (Gen. 33:9, 11).

It is as rare as it is pleasing to meet with a man who has enough; the great majority are craving for more. Here we see two persons who were content. Two brothers of dissimilar disposition, each saying "I have enough." Where shall we find two brothers like them?

I. HERE IS AN UNGODLY MAN WHO HAS ENOUGH.

Because Esau has other faults, there is no necessity that he should be discontented and grasping: contentment is a moral excellence as much as a spiritual grace.

1. Yet it has its evil side.
It tends to breed a contempt for spiritual riches.
It may thus be a sign of having one's portion in this life.

II. HERE IS A GODLY MAN WHO HAS ENOUGH.

1. It is a pity that this is not true of every Christian man. Some appear to be eager after the world though they profess to be separated from it.

2. It is delightful to have enough. Contentment surpasses riches.

3. It is pleasant to have somewhat to spare for the poor; and this should be the aim of our labor. (Eph. 4:28).

4. It is best of all to have all things. In the margin we read that Jacob said, "I have all things." "All things are yours." (I Cor. 3:22).

C. H. SPURGEON'S SERMON NOTES
Edited and Condensed by David Otis Fuller
ZONDERVAN PUBLISHING HOUSE

* * * * *

WHO IS ON THE LORD'S SIDE?
Exodus 32:26

The incident in Israel's history. Satan vs. God for a nation. The Jews were left alone (Joshua; Elijah; Jesus; Paul).

I. THE CONFLICT OF SATAN VS. GOD TODAY.

Two very distinct lines, although moderns have lost sight of the fact.

II. WHO IS NOT ON THE LORD'S SIDE?

1. The out-and-out sinner.
2. The disobedient, drifting, unconcerned, indifferent Christian.
3. The ungrateful and insensitive.

III. WHY BE ON THE LORD'S SIDE?

1. The devil is a tyrant—God is the Liberator.
2. The side of truth, of virtue, of purity, of decency, of righteousness, of clean living.
3. The strongest, the happiest, the most useful, the safest, the eventually victorious side.
4. It brings great rewards here and hereafter.

IV. WHAT IS EXPECTED OF THOSE ON THE LORD'S SIDE?
(Luke 9:23)

1. A complete forsaking of the other side. Cannot serve God and mammon, Christ and the world.
2. A definite espousal of God and His cause.
3. A surrendered, obedient, public consecration of time, talents, money, lives.
4. A continuous communion with the Captain in prayer, in Bible study, in church work.
5. A ceaseless fight to the death vs. sin.
6. A striving, burning, yearning desire to see others won to Christ.

V. WHEN SHOULD WE ANSWER GOD'S APPEAL?

1. The obligation of personal consecration.
2. The obligation of renouncing earthly ties, so far as inconsistent with the higher allegiance.
3. The obligation of doing the Lord's work.

APPELMAN'S SERMON OUTLINES AND ILLUSTRATIONS
by
HYMAN J. APPELMAN

RELIGIOUS INDECISION

And Elijah came unto all the people, and said, How long halt ye between two opinions? if the Lord be God, follow him: but if Baal, then follow him. And the people answered him not a word (I Kings 18:21).

This text is taken from a story that presents a dramatic contest between Elijah and the prophets of Baal. It was an hour of destiny. This contest furnishes the basis for an appeal to both the friends and the enemies of God. It is an appeal suited to any people anywhere. It emphasizes the solemn fact that religion requires decision. No one can afford to be undecided about his religion. Let us consider such indecision in detail.

I. IT IS UNREASONABLE.

1. It is reasonable for the creature to serve the Creator. God gave us our existence. He sustains our lives. We could not live without Him. We owe something to Him. It is unreasonable not to follow Him.

2. It is reasonable to prepare for the future in this present life. We prepare for the future of this life in such things as food, clothing, home, etc. It is unreasonable not to prepare for eternity.

3. It is reasonable for a sinner to trust Christ. There is abundant testimony in the witness of millions of trustworthy Christians. They assure us of the faithfulness and the power of Christ to save. Everything is to be gained and nothing lost by putting our lives in His hands. It is unreasonable to distrust Him.

II. IT IS SINFUL.

1. God forbids it. To fail to make decision is to destroy God's Word. He calls us to choose "this day whom

ye will serve." To fail to make such a decision today is to put our opinion above God's. He says, "Now is the day of salvation." If we say "Not now," we ask God to yield in this matter to our wills. He says that such failure to choose is to choose against Him. Here, then, we face the matter of whose knowledge must be accepted and trusted.

III. IT IS DANGEROUS.

1. It is dangerous because every day it becomes more difficult to make a decision. Little by little the heart becomes hardened and less responsive to appeals.

2. It is dangerous because we may die without warning and thus be allowed no last-minute preparation. Delay plays with the soul as one might play with a diamond over deep water—a slip and it is lost forever. We could yield to the appeal of God and our Christian friends and not risk our souls to the despair of eternal separation from God.

3. It is dangerous because the Holy Spirit may leave us. God says, "My Spirit shall not always strive with man." In the Word of God we are taught that He sometimes gives us up to hardness of heart; also that "God shall send them strong delusion, that they should believe a lie: that they all might be damned." He threatens to laugh when their "fear cometh" and to refuse to hear when they call on Him, which is to say that the day of mercy may close. When the Spirit leaves us, there is no hope, and how soon He will make His departure is unknown. We should take no risks but decide for Christ now.

IV. Too Much Is Involved.

1. Our decision involves all eternity. If we do not choose to be His, we are voluntarily separating ourselves from Him. The consequences are of our own making.

2. To decide aright takes courage, but the heart assumes the responsibility of trusting itself to the only Savior.

3. Some will lament through all eternity their failure to to decide this question when an opportunity was afforded. It takes strength of character to decide to be a Christian. Those who do not decide will suffer eternal retribution. But all can, if they will, cease their indecision and with full purpose of mind and heart give themselves to the one eternal hope of the Christian faith. This is our appeal—that you accept Christ as your Savior.

SELECTED SERMON OUTLINES
by
J. B. TIDWELL

*   *   *   *   *

THE BLUNDERS OF A GREAT GENERAL

As seen in the story of Naaman (II Kings 5).

I. Wrong Price.
10 talents of silver, 6000 pieces of gold (v. 5), about equal to £16,000. Not enough (Luke 7:42).

II. Wrong Person.
"Send to the *King* of Israel" (v. 5) Maid said "prophet." Christ, God's Prophet alone can save today.

III. WRONG PLACE.
"Stood at the *door*" (v. 9). Almost there, but not altogether. So near, yet so far.

IV. WRONG PRESCRIPTION.
"I *thought* he would surely come out to me" (v. 11). Not thoughts, but acts. Prophet said, "*Go.*"

V. WRONG PASSION.
"He went away in a *rage*" (v. 12). But he turned again, went down, and was cleansed.

ONE THOUSAND SUBJECTS FOR SPEAKERS AND STUDENTS
by
Hy. Pickering
PICKERING & INGLIS LTD.

*   *   *   *   *

EYES OPENED

And Elisha prayed, and said, Lord, I pray thee, open his eyes, that he may see. And the Lord opened the eyes of the young men; and he saw: and, behold, the mountain was full of horses and chariots of fire round about Elisha (II Kings 6:17).

I. THE NATURAL EYE IS BLIND TO HEAVENLY THINGS.

God is everywhere; yet sin-blinded eyes see Him not.

Men themselves are evil, guilty, fallen; yet they see not their own wounds, and bruises, and putrefying sores.

This want of spiritual discernment makes man ignoble.

Samson blinded is a sorry spectacle; from a judge in Israel he sinks to a slave in Philistia.

This keeps a man content with the world; he does not see

how poor a thing it is, for which he sweats, and smarts, and sins, and sacrifices heaven.

This places men in danger. "If the blind lead the blind, both shall fall into the ditch" (Matt. 15:14).

II. God Alone Can Open Man's Eyes.

We can lead the blind, but we cannot make them see; we can put truth before them, but we cannot open their eyes; that work remains with God alone.

Some use artificial eyes, others try spectacles, telescopes, colored glasses, etc., but all in vain, while the eyes are blind. The cure is of the Lord alone.

1. To give sight is the same wonder as creation. Who can make an eye? In the sinner the faculty of spiritual vision is gone.

2. The man is born blind. His darkness is part of himself (John 9:32).
   Satan counterfeited this in the garden when he said, "Your eyes shall be opened, and ye shall be as gods" (Gen. 3:5).

III. We May Pray Him To Open Men's Eyes.

We ought to cry, "Lord, I pray thee, open his eyes, that he may see."

1. When we hear them inquiring, we should inquire of the Lord for them. Their prayer should call up ours.

2. The prayers of others availed for us, and therefore we ought to repay the blessing to the prayer-treasury of the church.

3. It will glorify God to open their eyes; let us pray with great expectancy, believing that He will honor His Son.

IV. GOD DOES OPEN MEN'S EYES.

1. He has done it in a moment. Notice the many miracles performed by our Lord on blind men.

2. He can open *your* eyes. Many are the forms of blindness, but they are all comprehended in that grand statement, "The Lord openeth the eyes of the blind" (Ps. 146:8).

V. EVEN THOSE WHO SEE NEED MORE SIGHT.

1. In the Scriptures more is to be seen. "Open Thou mine eyes, that I may behold wondrous things out of Thy law" (Ps. 119:18).

2. In the great doctrines of the gospel there is much latent light.

3. In Christ Jesus Himself there are hidden glories. "Sir, we would see Jesus" (John 12:21; Heb. 2:9).

C. H. SPURGEON'S SERMON NOTES
Edited and Condensed by David Otis Fuller, D. D.
ZONDERVAN PUBLISHING HOUSE

* * * * *

RUTH DECIDING FOR GOD

And Ruth said, Intreat me not to leave thee, or to return from following after thee: for whither thou goest I will go; and where thou lodgest, I will lodge: thy people shall be my people, and thy God my God (Ruth 1:16).

This is a brave, outspoken confession of faith, and it is made by a woman, a young woman, a poor woman, a widow woman, a foreigner.

I. AFFECTION FOR THE GODLY SHOULD INFLUENCE US TO GODLINESS.

Many forces combine to effect this:

1. There is the influence of companionship. We ought to be affected by godly people more than we are by the wicked, since we should lend ourselves to their influence.

2. The influence of admiration. Imitation is the most sincere praise; what we favor we follow. Let us therefore copy the saints.

3. The influence of fear of separation. It will be an awful thing to be eternally divided from the dear ones who seek our salvation; it is even painful to have to leave them at the Lord's Table, when they partake and we do not.

II. RESOLVES TO GODLINESS WILL BE TESTED.

1. By counting the cost. You yourself will have to come out from your friends, as Ruth did. You will have to share the lot of God's people, as Ruth shared with Naomi. (Heb. 11:24, 26).

2. By the duties involved in religion. Ruth must work in the fields. Some proud people will not submit to the rules of Christ's house, nor to the regulations which govern the daily lives of believers.

3. By the apparent coldness of believers. Naomi does not persuade her to keep with her, but the reverse. She was a prudent woman, and did not wish Ruth to come with her by persuasion, but by conviction.

III. Such Godliness Must Mainly Lie in the Choice of God.

1. This is the believer's distinguishing possession. "Thy God shall be my God."
2. His great article of belief. "I believe in God."
3. His trust and stay. (See Ruth 2:12). "This God is our God forever and ever, He will be our guide even unto death" (Ps. 48:14).

IV. But It Should Involve the Choice of His People.

A near Kinsman is among them. The true Boaz is willing to take us to Himself, and to redeem our inheritance.

Let us make deliberate, humble, firm, joyful, immediate choice for God and His saints; accepting their lodging in this world, and going with them whither they are going.

C. H. SPURGEON'S SERMON NOTES
Edited and Condensed by David Otis Fuller, D. D.
ZONDERVAN PUBLISHING HOUSE

* * * * *

PRECIOUS TRIALS

But when he hath tried me, I shall come forth as gold
(Job 23:10).

I. Trial Is a Divine Process.

1. God's will appoints them.
2. God's love effects them.
3. God's presence comforts in them.

II. Trial Is a Useful Process.

1. It is a token of value.
2. It is a test of genuineness.
3. It is a medium of purification.
4. It is a preparation for service.

PULPIT GERMS
by
Rev. W. W. Wythe
J. B. Lippincott Company

* * * * *

REBELLING AGAINST THE LIGHT

They are of those that rebel against the light
(Job 24:13).

These evidently had the light, and this should be esteemed as no small privilege, since to wander on the dark mountains is a terrible curse. Yet this privilege may turn into an occasion of evil.

Light has a sovereignty in it, so that to resist it is to rebel against it. God has given it to be a display of Himself, for God is light; and He has clothed it with a measure of His majesty and power of judgment.

Rebellion against light has in it a high degree of sin. It might be virtue to rebel against darkness, but what shall be said of those who withstand the light? resisting truth, holiness and knowledge?

I. Detect the Rebels.

Well-instructed persons, who have been accustomed to teach others, and yet turn aside to evil; these are grievous traitors. Children of Christian parents who sin against their early training; upon whom prayer and entreaty, precept and example are thrown away. Hearers of the word, who quench convictions deliberately, frequently, and with violence.

II. Describe the Forms of This Rebellion.

Some refuse light, being unwilling to know more than would be convenient; therefore they deny themselves time for thought, absent themselves from sermons, neglect godly reading, shun pious company, avoid reproof, etc.

Others scoff and fight against it, calling light darkness, and darkness light.   Infidelity, ribaldry, persecution, and such like, become their resort and shelter.

Many darken it for others, hindering its operations among men, hiding their own light under a bushel, ridiculing the efforts of others, etc.

III.   DECLARE THE FOLLY OF THIS REBELLION.

Light is our best friend, and it is wisdom to obey it; to resist it is to rebel against our own interest.

Light triumphs still.   Owls hoot, but the moon shines. Opposition to truth and righteousness is useless; it may even promote that which it aims to prevent.

Light would lead to more light.   Consent to it, for it will be beneficial to your own soul.

Light would lead to heaven, which is the center of light.

C. H. SPURGEON'S SERMON NOTES
Edited and Condensed by David Otis Fuller, D. D.
ZONDERVAN PUBLISHING HOUSE

* * * * *

THREE STEPS IN THE PRAYER LIFE
Psalm 5:1-7

I.   THE PRAYER'S REQUEST (verse 1).

1.   He hears every word we speak in even ordinary everyday conversation.

2.   How often we grieve Him!

3.   He hears also our *thoughts!*   Oh, how that startles and humbles us!

4.   But the Psalmist has particularly prayer in His mind.

5. He hears our prayers when offered audibly or inaudibly.

II. THE PRAYER'S DETERMINATION AS SELF-PRESERVATION (verses 2 and 3).

1. Come what may, "Unto Thee will I pray."
2. And one thing that makes him most determined to pray is the fact of the holiness of God (verse 4).
3. By prayer I receive strength to avoid and gain victory over evil and temptation.
4. And thus live and dwell in His Presence.
5. He determined to pray specially in the morning for "well begun is half done." And after prayer, continue all day to "look up!"

III. THE PRAYER ATTITUDE (verse 7).

1. He would not approach God on the ground of his own goodness, but rely on His mercy (Note, "multitude of Thy mercy").
2. And he would approach God in reverence. "And in Thy fear."

HANDFULS ON PURPOSE
Series XI
by
Robert Lee
PICKERING & INGLIS LTD.

*   *   *   *   *

WILDERNESS PROVISION IN PSALM 23
The Lord is my shepherd, I shall not want.

I. I SHALL NOT WANT REST.
Verse 2—He maketh me to lie down in green pastures.

II. I SHALL NOT WANT REFRESHMENT.
Verse 2—He leadeth me beside the still waters.

III. I SHALL NOT WANT RESTORATION.
Verse 3—He restoreth my soul.

IV. I SHALL NOT WANT COUNSEL.
Verse 3—He leadeth me in the paths of righteousness.

V. I SHALL NOT WANT COMPANIONSHIP.
Verse 4—For Thou art with me.

VI. I SHALL NOT WANT COMFORT.
Verse 4—Thy rod and Thy staff, they comfort me.

VII. I SHALL NOT WANT PROVENDER.
Verse 5—Thou preparest a table before me.

VIII. I SHALL NOT WANT POWER.
Verse 5—Thou anointest my head with oil.

IX. I SHALL NOT WANT ANYTHING HERE.
Verse 6—Goodness and mercy shall follow me all the days of my life.

X. I SHALL NOT WANT ANYTHING HEREAFTER.
Verse 6—I will dwell in the House of the Lord forever.

TWELVE BASKETS FULL OF ORIGINAL OUTLINES
AND SCRIPTURE STUDIES
Compiled by Hy. Pickering
PICKERING & INGLIS LTD.

* * * * *

THE LORD OUR REFUGE

The Lord is my strength and my shield (Ps. 28:7).

I. THE LORD ACKNOWLEDGED.

1. As the source of strength.
    (a) Physical. (b) Intellectual. (c) Spiritual.

2. As a shield.
    Against temptation, the fiery darts of Satan, and the attacks of personal enemies.

II. THE LORD TRUSTED.
1. With the heart.
2. For the salvation of the soul.
3. For the power to keep from falling.
4. For help in every hour of need.

III. THE LORD REJOICED IN.
1. Because the soul is at peace with God.
2. Because of the consciousness of security in God.
3. Because of the manifested presence of God in the soul.

IV. THE LORD PRAISED.
1. For the manifestation of His power.
   (a) To give strength in the hour of weakness.
   (b) To give encouragement in the hour of despondency.
   (c) To give light in the hour of darkness.
   (d) To give inspiration in the hour of conflict.

2. For the manifestation of His love.
   (a) In cleansing the heart from all sin.
   (b) In inscribing the name in heaven.
   (c) In the adoption of sons into the Divine family.
   (d) In the blessed assurance of an eternal home in heaven.

THE SEED BASKET FOR PREACHERS AND TEACHERS
FRANK J. BOYER, PUBLISHER

*   *   *   *   *

"IN ALL THY WAYS"

For he shall give his Angels charge over thee, to keep thee is all thy Ways (Psalm 91:11).

The Lord gave his people shelter in the time of pestilence, for he had promised, "There shall no evil befall thee;

neither shall any plague come nigh thy dwelling." The former verses celebrate the Passover of those who dwell in God.

After the Passover came a journey to Canaan; and the promise of the covenant angel and his keeping them in all their ways, fitly follow upon the rescue from the plague.

We, too, are pilgrims on our way to Canaan. He who set us free by the Passover deliverance also provides for our journey to the land which floweth with milk and honey. All the way to the promised land is covered by this divine safe-conduct.

I. THERE ARE WAYS WHICH ARE NOT IN THE PROMISE.

"All thy ways," are mentioned; but some tracks are not to be followed by children of God, and are not their ways.

1. Ways of presumption. In these men court danger, and as it were, defy God. "Cast thyself down," said Satan to our Lord, and then urged this promise (Matt. 4:6).

2. Ways of sin, dishonesty, lying, vice, worldly conformity, etc. We have no permit to bow in the house of Rimmon (Eph. 5:12).

3. Ways of worldliness, selfishness, greed, ambition. The ways by which men seek personal aggrandizement are usually dark and crooked, and are not of God (Prov. 28:22; I Tim. 6:9).

4. Ways of pride, self-conceit, boastful promising, pretended perfection, etc. "Pride goeth before destruction."

5. Ways of will-worship, wilfulness, obstinacy, fancy, day-dreaming, absurd impulse, etc. (Jer. 2:18).

6. Ways of erroneous doctrine, novel practice, fashionable ceremonial, flattering delusion, etc. (II Tim. 3:5).

II. THERE ARE WAYS IN WHICH SAFETY IS GUARANTEED.
   1. The way of humble faith in the Lord Jesus.
   2. The way of obedience to divine precepts.
   3. The way of childlike trust in providential guidance.
   4. The way of strict principle and stern integrity.
   5. The way of consecrated service, and seeking God's glory.
   6. The way of holy separation, and walking with God.

III. THESE WAYS LEAD US INTO VARIED CONDITIONS.
   1. They are changeful and varied: "all thy ways."
   2. They are sometimes stony with difficulty: "foot against a stone."
   3. They may be terrible with temptation.
   4. They may be mysteriously trying. Devils may throng the path, only to be met by holy angels.
   5. They are essentially safe, while the smooth and easy roads are perilous.

IV. BUT WHILE WALKING IN THEM ALL BELIEVERS ARE SECURE.
   1. The Lord himself concerns himself about them: *"He shall give his angels charge over thee."* He will personally command those holy beings to have an eye to his children. David charged his troops to spare Absalom, but his bidding was disregarded. It is not so with God.
   2. Mysterious agencies protect them: angels bear them up in their hands, as nurses carry little children. Wonderful tenderness and power: angels acting as servants to men!
   3. All things are on their side, both visible and invisible. Command is laid on all to protect the saints. "Thou hast given commandment to save me" (Psa. 71:3).

4. Each one is personally watched over. "Charge over *thee* to keep *thee*" (Isa. 42:6; Gen. 28:15).

5. That watchfulness is perpetual—"All thy ways" (Psa. 121:3, 4).

6. This guard also confess honor. How noble a thing to have the courtiers of heaven for a *corps de garde!*

7. All this comes to them by Jesus, whose the angels are, and whom they serve (Isa. 43:4).

See how the lowest employment is consistent with the highest enjoyment. Keeping guard over the Lord's stumbling children is no discredit to angels.

How cheerfully we should watch over others! How vigorously should we hold them up whenever it is in our power. To cast off a stumbling brother is not angelic, but the reverse.

How safe we ought to feel, how fully trustful we ought to be. Alexander slept soundly, "for," said he, "Parmenio wakes."

How holy we should be with such holy ones for watchers! Great privileges involve heavy responsibilities.

MY SERMON-NOTES
by
C. H. Spurgeon
FLEMING H. REVELL COMPANY

* * * * *

LIGHTS AND LAMPS FOR ALL
Thy Word is a lamp (Psalm 119:105).

Electric Stove

Many kinds of lamps for many different uses in many different places, yet all to give light.

So the Bible lamp is always light-giving in many different circumstances of life.

*word of God—Lamp giving light
in many ways Directions*

I. As a Hurricane Lamp.

Never blown out. Been proved by opposition, fire and persecution.

II. As a Beacon Lamp.

Continually giving light, saving thousands of lives, guiding them into a port of safety.

III. As a Signal Lamp. → *this is my walk ye in it.*

Points the right road, with encouragements to go on, sometimes with caution and care (green light), as danger is near (red light). If these lights were more heeded there would be less sorrow in the world.

IV. As an Invalid's Lamp. → *for sick & weary*

Not left in the dark; a mellow light in sick room gives cheer and company. So the Bible with its sweet, cheery messages gives comfort to the sick and weary.

V. As a Worker's Lamp.

Much work is done by night-light in rescuing the perishing and fallen. Need of light where darkness and evil abound.

VI. As a Pilgrim's Lamp.

Needful, for rough and rocky is the road sometimes. Life is an unknown road.

Nobody ever outgrows the Bible; the book widens and deepens with our years.

THE PREACHER'S AND TEACHER'S VADE-MECUM
Compiled by J. Ellis
ALLENSON & CO. LIMITED

* * * * *

A MESSAGE TO YOUNG MEN

My son, if sinners entice thee, consent thou not (Prov. 1:10).

In this chapter, verses 10 to the end, we have set before us the seduction and destruction of young men and women.

I. THE SEDUCTION.   (To entice—to persuade).

  1. *The Seduced.* All are in danger; all are tempted; but young people are in greatest danger:

    (a) because of inexperience, ignorance.

    (b) because of the desperate efforts made on the part of men and demons to destroy our youth.

    (c) because of the many traps and pitfalls: theaters, saloons, clubs, dance halls, bad books, etc.

    (d) because of lack of protection:—Home protection —Church protection.

  2. *The Seducers*—(sinners)

  All unsaved are sinners; all who deviate from the path of righteousness; all have influence; no one goes to destruction alone; some sinners have more influence than others:—

    (a) those in authority—a master, a father, a king. Jeroboam drove Israel to sin.

    (b) those who pose as friends.

    (c) those who have personal attractions: learned, witty, intellectual, bad men.

    (d) those who have personal influence, wealth, social distinction, etc.

  3. *The Seducing.* The methods used:—

    (a) persuasiveness—"entice" v. 10.

    (b) amalgamation—"come with us" v. 11.

    (c) remuneration—"fill our houses with spoil" v. 13.

    (d) sociability—"one purse" v. 14.

II. DESTRUCTION.

Having refused a father's instruction, a mother's pleas, and the Spirit's wooing, vs. 20-23, there remaineth naught but destruction. Note—

  1. "I will laugh at your *calamity*."

5 2 8

2. "I will mock when your *fear* cometh."

3. I will not answer, and that when desolation, destruction, distress and anguish cometh (v. 27).

"PREACH THE WORD"

by

Rev. Frederick Rader

ECONOMY PRINTING CONCERN

*   *   *   *   *

INVITATION TO A CONFERENCE

> Come now, and let us reason together, saith the Lord: though your sins be as scarlet, they shall be as white as snow; though they be red like crimson, they shall be as wool (Isaiah 1:18).

The sinful condition of men is terrible in the extreme. This is set forth vividly in previous verses of the chapter. They are altogether alienated from their God.

I. AN INVITATION TO A CONFERENCE.

Sinful men do not care to think, consider, and look matters in the face, yet to this distasteful duty they are urged.

If they reason, they rather reason against God than together with Him; but here the proposal is not to discuss, but to treat with a view to reconciliation. This also ungodly hearts decline.

1. They prefer to attend to ceremonial observances. Outward performances are easier, and do not require thought.

2. Yet the matter is one which demands most serious discussion, and deserves it; for God, the soul, heaven, and hell are involved in it. Never was wise counsel more desirable.

3. It is most gracious on the Lord's part to suggest a conference. Kings do not often invite criminals to reason with them.

4. The invitation is a pledge that He desires peace, is willing to forgive, and anxious to set us right.

II. A SPECIMEN OF THE REASONING ON GOD'S PART.

1. The one main ground of difference is honestly mentioned—"though your sins be as scarlet." God calls the most glaring sinners to come to Him, knowing them to be such.

2. This ground of difference God Himself will remove—"they shall be as white as snow." He will forgive, and so end the quarrel.

3. He will remove the offence perfectly—"as snow—as wool."
   He will remove forever the guilt of sin.
   He will discharge the penalty of sin.
   He will destroy the dominion of sin.
   He will prevent the return of sin.

III. THIS SPECIMEN REASONING IS AN ABSTRACT OF THE WHOLE ARGUMENT.

Each special objection is anticipated.

1. The singular greatness of your sins,—"red like crimson." This is met by a great atonement, which cleanses from all sin.

2. The long continuance of your sins. Cloth dyed scarlet has lain long in the dye-vat. The blood of Jesus cleanses at once.

3. The light against which your sins were committed. This puts a glaring color upon them. But "all manner of sin and blasphemy shall be forgiven unto men."

4. The despair which your sins create: they are so glaring that they are ever before you, yet they shall be washed out by the blood of the Lamb of God, which taketh away the sin of the world.

C. H. SPURGEON'S SERMON NOTES
Edited and Condensed by David Otis Fuller, D. D.
ZONDERVAN PUBLISHING HOUSE

* * * * *

SOUR GRAPES
Ezekiel 18

The moral of the well-known proverb "The fathers have eaten sour grapes, and the children's teeth are set on edge" is simply this: When the fathers sin, the children suffer.

The proverb should be set aside and personal responsibility fixed: "The soul that sinneth, it shall die" (verse 4).

God has no pleasure in the death of the wicked (verse 32), and He sends out an earnest appeal: "Why will ye die?" Beginning with the last word, we will consider each word as a question.

I. DIE?

Obviously the term does not refer to physical death, which is inevitable, but eternal death, which is escapable. It is called "the second death" and is the final issue of sin. It is not extinction of being, thought, feeling, memory, etc. The rich man in hell had all these faculties in active operation. He saw; he felt; he remembered; he thought; he prayed. This death means exclusion from heaven; separation from God and all that is good and joyous; companionship with the devil and his angels in a place "where torment no end shall know, though briny tears forever flow."

II. YE?

The prophet was speaking to the house of Israel, a favored

people surrounded with privileges, the descendants of the fathers, a people to whom were committed the oracles of God. Yet it was possible for many of them to die death in which God had no pleasure.

It is sad to think of the heathen dying in darkness, but it is even sadder to think of people who have been born in lands where the Bible is read and the Gospel preached but who are nevertheless dying without Christ.

III. WILL?

Whoever dies and is lost wills it to be so. "God willeth not the death of any." "Wilt thou be made whole?" is the question of our Lord to us. Everything depends upon the will. "Ye will not come to me, that ye might have life." "I would, but ye would not." The hymn writer expressed this well when he wrote:

> Let your will to God be given,
>   Trust in Christ's atoning blood;
> Look to Jesus now in heaven,
>   Rest on His unchanging Word.

IV. WHY?

Some will die in spite of God's love and the Gospel invitation.

1. Because they love sin.

2. Because they will not think of eternity.

3. Because they reject Christ.

PRACTICAL SERMON OUTLINES
by
J. B. TIDWELL

* * * * *

THE NAME OF JESUS

Thou shalt call His name Jesus, for He shall save His people from their sins (Matt. 1:21).

Almost every historic person in the Bible bears an appropriate name; thus the name came to be identified with the person. In this text the name Jesus is declared to be descriptive of the person and the work of Christ.

I. LET ME CALL YOUR ATTENTION TO THE SAVIOR.

Jesus signifies, Jehovah that saves. So Jesus is Divine: He saves His people from their sins. Not the word, not the ordinances, but Jesus Himself.

II. LOOK AT THE SALVATION.

1. Jesus saves from sin by bestowing forgiveness—full forgiveness, free, immediate, and irreversible.
2. Jesus saves His people from the pollution of sin; not in their sins, but from their sins. It is true that holiness is progressive, but the Christian cannot and does not love sin. Nor can he live in sin as the choice and habit of his life. This salvation shall be completed in heaven.

III. LET US LOOK AT THE SAVED.

"He shall save His people." Who are His people? They must have been at one time in their sins. Therefore no one need despair. "But does not the phrase speak of election? and how do I know that I am elected?" Your business is not with election but with your calling, and you may make your calling sure by believing. Whosoever believeth in Him shall not perish. "Whosoever!" Every one feels that includes him. "Whosoever believeth"; does that include you?

W. M. Taylor

THREE HUNDRED OUTLINES OF SERMONS
ON THE NEW TESTAMENT
JENNINGS & GRAHAM

* * * * *

ALONE WITH SATAN
Matt. 4:1-11
Introduction: A surprising passage and its real meaning.

I. SATAN'S ADVANTAGES.
   1. Forbidding surroundings.
   2. Isolation from his kind (Christ must go alone to meet the tempter).
   3. Physical exhaustion.

II. THE FOURFOLD TEST.
   1. Temptation to doubt.
   2. To misuse His power.
   3. To give way to spiritual pride.
   4. To give selfish ambition first place.

III. THE RESULT.
   Satan gave up the struggle because Jesus
   1. Met falsehood with the Word of truth.
   2. Used His will-power.
   3. Rebuked the tempter.

SERMON NOTES FROM THE MINISTRY OF JESUS
by
Mattie M. Boteler
THE STANDARD PUBLISHING COMPANY

* * * * *

SONSHIP QUESTIONED
If Thou be the Son of God (Matt. 4:3).

There is no sin in being tempted (Heb. 4:15).

Temptation does not necessitate sinning.

It may be needful for us to be tempted—
   For test. Sincerity, faith, love, patience, are thus put to proof. For usefulness. We become able to comfort and warn others.

Solitude will not prevent temptation.

It may even aid it. Jesus was tempted in the wilderness. Nor will fasting and prayer always keep off the tempter; for these had been fully used by our Lord.

Satan knows how to write prefaces: our text is one.

He began the whole series of his temptations by a doubt cast upon our Lord's Sonship, and a crafty quotation from Scripture.

I.   THE TEMPTER ASSAILS WITH AN "IF."

1. Not with point-blank denial. That would be too startling. Doubt serves the Satanic purpose better than heresy.
2. He ifs a plain Scripture. "Thou art my Son" (Ps. 2:7).
3. He ifs a whole life. From the first Jesus had been about His Father's business; yet after thirty years His Sonship is questioned.

II.   THE TEMPTER AIMS THE "IF" AT A VITAL PART.

1. At our sonship.
   In our Lord's case he attacks his human and divine Sonship.
   In our case he would make us doubt our regeneration.
2. At our Father's honor. He tempts us to doubt our Father's providence, and to blame Him for letting us hunger.

III.   THE TEMPTER SUPPORTS THAT "IF" WITH CIRCUMSTANCES.

1. You are alone. Would a Father desert His child?
2. You are in a desert. Is this the place for God's Heir?
3. You are with the wild beasts. Wretched company for a Son of God!
4. You are an hungered. How can a loving Father let His perfect Son hunger?

Put all these together, and the tempter's question comes home with awful force to one who is hungry, and alone.

When we see others thus tried, do we think them brethren? Do we not question their sonship, as Job's friends questioned him? What wonder if we question ourselves!

IV. WHEN OVERCOME, THE TEMPTER'S "IF" IS HELPFUL.

   1. As coming from Satan, it is a certificate of our true descent.

      He only questions *truth:* therefore we are true sons.

      He only leads *sons* to doubt their sonship; therefore we are sons.

   2. It takes the sting out of man's questionings and suspicions; for if we have answered the devil we do not fear men.

   3. As past, it is usually the prelude to angels coming and ministering to us, as in our Lord's case. No calm is so deep as that which follows a great storm (Mark 4:39).

C. H. SPURGEON'S SERMON NOTES

Edited and Condensed by David Otis Fuller, D. D.

ZONDERVAN PUBLISHING HOUSE

*   *   *   *   *

THE MAKING OF MEN-CATCHERS

And He said unto them, Follow Me, and I will make you fishers of men (Matthew 4: 19).

Conversion is most fully displayed when it leads converts to seek the conversion of others: we must truly follow Christ when we become fishers of men.

I. SOMETHING TO BE DONE BY US. "FOLLOW ME."

   1. We must be separated to Him that we may pursue His object.

We cannot follow Him unless we leave others (Matt. 6:24).

2. We must abide with Him, that we may catch His spirit.

3. We must obey Him that we may learn His method.
   Teach what He taught (Matt. 28:20).
   Teach as He taught (Matt. 11:29; I Thess. 2:7).
   Teach such as He taught, namely, the poor, the base, children, etc.

II. SOMETHING TO BE DONE BY HIM. "I WILL MAKE YOU."

1. By our following Jesus He works conviction and conversion in men; He uses our example as a means to this end.

2. By His Spirit He qualifies us to reach men.

3. By His secret working on men's hearts He speeds us in our work.

III. A FIGURE INSTRUCTING US. "FISHERS OF MEN."

The man who saves souls is like a fisher upon the sea.

1. A fisher is dependent and trustful.
2. He is diligent and persevering.
3. He is intelligent and watchful.
4. He is laborious and self-denying.
5. He is daring, and is not afraid to venture upon a dangerous sea.
6. He is successful. He is no fisher who never catches anything.

C. H. SPURGEON'S SERMON NOTES
Edited and Condensed by David Otis Fuller, D. D.
ZONDERVAN PUBLISHING HOUSE

* * * * *

THE CHRISTIAN MOTIVE
For My sake (Matt. 5:11).

The words specially bring before us the relation of the Christian to his living and loving Lord.

I. LET US SEEK TO GET A CLEARER VIEW OF THE INFLUENCE OF THE CHRISTIAN MOTIVE.

The Lord Jesus has certain special and peculiar claims on us.

There is the authority of His Godhead, and the love of His incarnation and death.

II. LET US SEEK TO GET A JUSTER ESTIMATE OF ITS RANGE.

1. It bears with full force on our efforts after personal holiness.
2. It bears with great effect on the Christian's work for others.
3. The principle extends to the enduring of suffering for conscience sake.
4. It applies with great force to the sacrifices we are required to make.

This principle has a testing power in it which will reveal whether or not we are as we profess to be, the followers of Christ.   *W. M. Taylor*

THREE HUNDRED OUTLINES OF SERMONS
ON THE NEW TESTAMENT
JENNINGS & GRAHAM

* * * * *

WITH JESUS THROUGH THE STORM
Matt. 8:23-27

Introduction: The settings of the story: a day of strenuous work and of public and private teaching.

I. THE WEARY SLEEPER.
   1. A manifestation of the genuineness of His humanity.
   2. The wearing nature of His work.

II. AN UNEXPECTED STORM.
   Why it was permitted to come, since
   1. He who afterward quelled the storm was with them.
   2. They were following Jesus.

III. THE DISCIPLES.
   1. They were frightened at the fury of the storm.
   2. They were impatient with Jesus.
   3. They were distrustful.

IV. THEY WERE SHORT-SIGHTED.
   1. They had forgotten past manifestations of His power.
   2. He was sharing the same danger that they were.

V. THE EFFECT OF HIS WORDS.
   The storm ceased; the fearful were made confident.

SERMON NOTES FROM THE MINISTRY OF JESUS
by
Mattie M. Boteler
THE STANDARD PUBLISHING COMPANY

*   *   *   *   *

CROSS-BEARING

He that taketh not his cross and followeth after Me, is
not worthy of Me (Matthew 10:38).

Picture to the mind's eye a procession led by a cross-bearing Jesus, and made up of His cross-bearing train. This is not a pageant, but a real march of suffering. It reaches through all time.

Let us obediently inquire—

I. WHAT IS MY PECULIAR CROSS?
"He that taketh not *his* cross."

1. It may be the endurance of reproach and unkindness, or remaining in poverty and obscurity for the good of others.
2. It may be the suffering of losses and persecutions, for Christ's sake.
3. It certainly means the consecrating of all to Jesus, the bowing of my whole self beneath the blessed burden of service with which He honors me.

II. WHAT AM I TO DO WITH IT?

"Taketh . . . followeth after Me."

1. I am deliberately to take it up.
   Not to choose a cross, or pine after another form of trial.
   Not to make a cross by petulance and obstinacy.
   Not to murmur at the cross appointed me.
   Not to despise it, by callous stoicism, or wilful neglect of duty.
   Not to faint under it, fall beneath it, or run from it.
2. I am boldly to face it. It is only a wooden cross after all.
3. I am patiently to endure it, for I have only to carry it a little way.
4. I am cheerfully to resign myself to it, for my Lord appoints it.

It is a royal burden, a sanctified burden, a sanctifying burden, a burden which gives communion with Christ.

III. WHAT SHOULD ENCOURAGE ME?

1. Necessity: I cannot be a disciple without cross-bearing.
2. Society: better men than I have carried it.
3. Love: Jesus bore a far heavier cross than mine.
4. Faith: grace will be given equal to the weight of the cross.

5. Expectation: glory will be the reward of it. No cross, no crown.

C. H. SPURGEON'S SERMON NOTES
Edited and Condensed by David Otis Fuller, D. D.
ZONDERVAN PUBLISHING HOUSE

*   *   *   *   *

LEARNING OF CHRIST
Learn of Me (Matt. 11: 29).

Jesus is the Great Teacher, but that will be of no avail unless we are also great learners. We may "learn of," or, as the word means, "from Christ,"—

I. BY LISTENING TO HIS DIRECT TEACHINGS.

As a teacher Jesus is authoritative. He made statements regarding things—those of the unseen world, for instance—which were to be received because He made them. Yet He never frowned upon inquiry into the truth of what He taught.

II. BY CONTEMPLATING HIS CHARACTER WE LEARN OF CHRIST.

Teaching by precept and teaching by example has each its place, but the teaching of the latter is the more attractive. In Jesus we see everything that belongs to the ideal excellence of our nature, so that to be Christlike is to be perfect.

III. WE LEARN OF CHRIST FROM THE PRACTICAL EXPERIENCES OF THE CHRISTIAN LIFE.

To get the full benefit of Christ's teaching, it is not enough that we "sit at His feet and hear His words." There must be the taking up of His yoke, which is easy, and His burden, which is light. There must be the growing like Christ, as well as the gaining of acquaintance with His life. The whole every-day practice of our religion is a constant learning of Christ, just as the constant practice of speaking and writing is the learning of a language.

It is written that "he that increaseth knowledge increaseth sorrow," but the happy effect of "learning of Christ" is that we "find rest to our souls."

Walter Morrison

THREE HUNDRED OUTLINES OF SERMONS
ON THE NEW TESTAMENT
JENNINGS & GRAHAM

* * * * *

THE SOWER

Behold, a sower went forth to sow (Matt. 13:3).

I. THE SEED.
1. God's Word.
   a. Prophecies.
   b. Promises.
   c. Doctrines.
2. Christ's Gospel.
   a. His discourses.
   b. His life.
   c. His death.
   d. His resurrection.
3. All truth is living seed.

II. THE GROUND.
1. Its variety.
   a. Hard.
   b. Stony.
   c. Thorny.
   d. Good.
2. The heart.
3. The thoughts.

4. The memory.
5. The affections.

III. THE SOWERS ENGAGED.
1. Preachers.
2. Teachers.
3. Guardians.
4. Children of God.

IV. THE GROWTH OF THE CORN.
1. The blade, ear, full corn.
2. Attention, prayer, obedience.

V. THE HARVEST HOME.
1. Sunshine, golden grain.
2. Gladness for plenty.
3. Harvest of a good life; gathering truth from—
   a. Creation.
   b. Providence.
   c. Revelation.
   d. Experience.
4. The fruit of the Spirit is the rich harvest of eternal life.

SERMONS IN A NUTSHELL
by
J. ELLIS

*   *   *   *   *

THE UNCLEAN SPIRIT
Mark 1:21-27

Jesus had gone into Capernaum. On the quiet Sabbath day He makes His way to the synagogue, that He might declare the will of His Father in Heaven. Every opportunity of doing good is *straightway* accepted by our Lord. Instant in season. May His Holy Spirit work this good work in our hearts! Guided by the Holy Spirit, Jesus is brought into contact with an unclean spirit. It is a *day of grace* for the poor demon-possessed man. Notice His—

I. CHARACTER.

"A man with an *unclean* spirit," or we may read it, "A man *in,* or being controlled by, an unclean spirit." A man in an unclean spirit is of course an unclean man.

II. POSITION.

"In their synagogue" on the Sabbath day. An unclean man keeping the Sabbath and reverencing the sanctuary. A religious devil. A man's outward acts do not always determine his moral character. It is possible to have the *form* of godliness while denying the power. Unclean spirits may go regularly to the house of God.

III. QUESTION.

"What have we to do with Thee, Thou Jesus of Nazareth?" Just so. These unclean worshippers have nothing to do with Jesus. This evil spirit cries out, "What have *we* to do with Thee?" The man and the unclean spirit are as one.

IV. CONFESSION.

"I know Thee who Thou art, the Holy One of God." Why does he not say *we* know Thee? This demon speaks for himself, and betrays a knowledge far superior to the poor devil-driven man. Observe carefully his language, "Art Thou come to destroy *us;* I know *Thee.*" Jesus came not to destroy, but to save.

V. REQUEST.

"Let us alone." Although these words do not appear in the Revised Version, they doubtless express the deep-rooted desire of every unclean spirit. Every sin-loving sinner wishes to be *let alone* by the Holy One of God. They love the darkness rather than the light, because their deeds are evil. Well, if Jesus should let the unclean *alone,* what then? Just this, they will abide forever under the damning power of sin and Satan, cast out with the devil and his angels. Abide Thou with us.

VI. POWER.

"When the unclean spirit had *torn* him he cried." Beware of sin, it first cries, "Let alone," then tears in pieces. It has power to *pollute* and to destroy. Self is one of the most dangerous of all the seducing spirits. In the work of God it often is as a fly in the ointment. The spirit of uncleanness has *torn* the minds, hearts, and lives, and hopes of many to pieces, and would tear the very Word of God out of our hands.

VII. OVERCOMER.

Jesus rebuked him, saying, "Hold thy peace, and come out of him." He gagged him and cast him out. The unclean need to be rebuked, even when they talk religiously, saying, "Thou art the Holy One of God." It is easy for an unclean spirit to overcome an unholy man, but the presence and power of the Holy One is sufficient to silence and to separate.

HANDFULS ON PURPOSE
Series II
by
Pastor James Smith
PICKERING & INGLIS LTD.

* * * * *

GETHSEMANE

And they come to a place which was named Gethsemane (Mark 14:32).

It was a killing change from the cheerful communion of the Supper to the lone agony of the garden.

I. THE CHOICE OF THE SPOT.

1. Showed His serenity of mind, and His courage.

   He goes to His usual place of secret prayer.

   He goes there though Judas knew the place.

2. Manifested His wisdom.

Holy memories there aided His faith.

Deep solitude was suitable for His prayers and cries.

3. Bequeathed us lessons.

   In a garden, Paradise was lost and won.

   In Gethsemane, the olive-press, our Lord Himself was crushed.

II. THE EXERCISE UPON THE SPOT.

1. He took all due precautions for others.

   He would not have His disciples surprised, and therefore bade them watch.

2. He solicited the sympathy of friends.

   We may not despise this; though, like our Lord, we shall prove the feebleness of it, and cry, "Could ye not watch with Me?"

3. He prayed and wrestled with God.

   In lowliest posture and manner. (See verse 35).

   In piteous repetition of His cry. (See verses 36 and 39).

   In awful agony of spirit even to a bloody sweat (Luke 22:44).

4. He again and again sought human sympathy, but made excuse for His friends when they failed Him. (See verse 38). We ought not to be soured in spirit even when we are bitterly disappointed.

III. THE TRIUMPH UPON THE SPOT.

1. Behold His perfect resignation. He struggles with "If it be possible," but conquers with "not what I will, but what Thou wilt." He is our example of patience.

2. Mark the angelic service rendered. The Blood-bestained Sufferer has still all heaven at His call. (Matt. 26:53).

3. Remember His majestic bearing towards His enemies. He meets them bravely (Matt. 26:55).

He makes them fall (John 18:6).

He yields Himself, but not to force (John 18:8).

He goes to the cross but transforms it to a throne.

C. H. SPURGEON'S SERMON NOTES
Edited and Condensed by David Otis Fuller
ZONDERVAN PUBLISHING HOUSE

* * * * *

AT JESUS' FEET
The Woman of Luke 7: 37-46.

I. STOOD AT HIS FEET—In Confession.

II. WEPT AT HIS FEET—In Penitence.

III. WASHED HIS FEET—In Humiliation.

IV. WIPED HIS FEET—In Devotion.

V. KISSED HIS FEET—In Affection.

VI. ANOINTED HIS FEET—In Adoration.

FIVE HUNDRED SCRIPTURE OUTLINES
by
John Ritchie
JOHN RITCHIE, PUBLISHER

* * * * *

THE PARABLE OF THE GOOD SAMARITAN
Luke 10: 30

A CERTAIN MAN—the whole human race.

WENT DOWN—fell.

FROM JERUSALEM—the place of blessing.

"In Salem also is His tabernacle, and His dwelling place in Zion" (Ps. 76:2).

TO JERICHO—the place of the curse.

"And Joshua adjured them at that time, saying, Cursed be the man before the Lord, that riseth up and buildeth this city Jericho" (Josh. 6:26).

AND FELL AMONG THIEVES—Satan and his angels.

WHICH STRIPPED HIM OF HIS RAIMENT—Satan stripped man of his innocency.

AND WOUNDED HIM—a wound which brought death to mankind.

AND DEPARTED—having set man going, Satan could leave him on his path. "A child left to himself bringeth his mother to shame" (Prov. 29:15).

LEAVING HIM HALF DEAD—dead in soul, mortal in body.

AND BY CHANCE—that is, by coincidence.

A CERTAIN PRIEST—the law.

CAME DOWN THAT WAY—going the same downward path. "None of them can by any means redeem his brother" (Ps. 49:7).

AND WHEN HE SAW HIM, HE PASSED BY ON THE OTHER SIDE—unable or unwilling to help.

AND LIKEWISE A LEVITE—ceremonials.

BUT A CERTAIN SAMARITAN—Jesus incarnate.

AS HE JOURNEYED—it does not say *"down."*
Perhaps he was journeying up to Jerusalem.

CAME WHERE HE WAS—became "partaker of flesh and blood" (Heb. 2:14).

AND WHEN HE SAW HIM, HE HAD COMPASSION ON HIM—just as Jesus had when He saw the bereaved widow of Nain (Luke 7:13).

AND WENT TO HIM, AND BOUND UP HIS WOUNDS—"with his stripes we are healed,"—at Calvary.

POURING IN OIL AND WINE—at *Pentecost.*

AND SET HIM ON HIS OWN BEAST—putting man in His own place. "And hath raised us up together, and made us sit together in heavenly places in Christ Jesus" (Eph. 2:6).

AND BROUGHT HIM TO AN INN—where all bonafide travelers were received.

AND TOOK CARE OF HIM—knowing the negligence of the servants.

AND ON THE MORROW WHEN HE DEPARTED—to return to heaven.

HE TOOK OUT TWO PENCE—two gifts.

AND GAVE THEM TO THE HOST—"But unto every one of us is given *grace* according to the measure of the *gift* of Christ" (Eph. 4:7).

AND SAID UNTO HIM, TAKE CARE OF HIM—"Bear ye one another's burdens, and so fulfil the law of Christ" (Gal. 6:2).

AND WHATSOEVER THOU SPENDEST OVER, I WILL REPAY THEE—no care shown to wounded travelers is forgotten. "And the King shall answer and say unto them, Verily I say unto you, Inasmuch as ye have done it unto one of the least of these my brethren, ye have done it unto me" (Matt. 25:40).

WHEN I COME AGAIN—His second coming.

NOTES FROM MY BIBLE
by D. L. Moody
THE BIBLE INSTITUTE COLPORTAGE

* * * * *

PICTURE OF LOVE AT HOME

A sister called Mary, which also sat at Jesus' feet
(Luke 10:39).

This family was highly favored by being permitted to entertain Christ so often. Mary made the wisest use of it.

Attending to His words, serving Him with her best love, and sitting at His feet. The good part chosen.

I. LOVE AT LEISURE.

At eventide round the fireside love rests and communes, forgetting care. Like Mary, we would feel quite at home with Jesus, free from worldly care, leaving all with Him; enjoying His finished work, the great gifts already received, and more to follow in due season (Rom. 8:32). Time, future, and eternity safe in Him. Leisure, not laziness, to love, commune, and copy.

II. LOVE IN LOWLINESS.

At Jesus' feet. Let me be a penitent—an acknowledgment of unworthiness; a disciple—a confession of ignorance; a receiver—an admission of emptiness.

III. LOVE LISTENING.

And hear His Word. Listen to what He says in His Word, in creation, providence, and by His Spirit. Study Him, not obtruding our own self-formed thoughts, notions, reasonings, questionings, desires, and prejudices.

IV. LOVE IN POSSESSION.

She had full enjoyment, perfect satisfaction, full assurance, and resolute constancy.

To be more with Jesus—this is true life.

To hear Jesus more—this is true service.

To love Jesus more—this is true treasure.

THE PREACHER'S AND TEACHER'S VADE-MECUM
ALLENSON & CO. LIMITED

* * * * *

FORGIVENESS OF SINS
Luke 11: 1-4

The forgiveness of sins is an experience which is—

I. REAL.
A solid and substantial thing. Nothing imaginary about it. It rests on the Death and Resurrection of the Lord Jesus Christ, and upon His word.

II. ELEMENTARY.
It is of first necessity to the sinner, the first experienced blessing of the Gospel.

III. VITAL.
Without it a man is not a Christian at all. It is fundamental to all other spiritual blessings, the very basis of Christian experience.

IV. COMPLETE.
It means more than being let off. It means "cutting off," excision. Forgiveness is a complete gift.

V. FRUITFUL.
Because of what follows, justification, peace, etc.

VI. REPEATED.
We need daily forgiveness, as our Lord taught in the Lord's Prayer.

THE OUTLINED ACTS
by
Robert Lee
PICKERING & INGLIS

* * * * *

THE MODEL PRAYER

And he said unto them, when ye pray, say, Our Father which art in heaven, Hallowed be thy name. Thy kingdom come. Thy will be done, as in heaven, so in earth (Luke 11:2).

In the prayer our Lord taught His disciples to pray we have all the conditions of prevailing prayer.

I. REGENERATION. *"Our Father."*

II. HUMILIATION. *"Which art in heaven."*

III. ADORATION. *"Hallowed be thy name."*

Our inmost souls cry out "Let God be honored," adored, loved, worshipped and revered on earth; all irreverent praying is mockery.

IV. SUPPLICATION. *"Thy kingdom come."*

The spiritual kingdom in the heart, and His eternal kingdom on earth.

That we do all we can to promote this great end.

V. CONSECRATION. *"Thy will be done."*

Ready to do God's will, instantly, willingly, wholly, constantly.

VI. SOLICITATION. *"Give us this day our daily bread."*

VII. RECONCILIATION. *"Forgive us our debts as we forgive our debtors."*

VIII. LIBERATION. *"Lead us not into temptation, but deliver us from evil."*

A fear and dread of sin—keep us from sinning against Thee.

IX. GLORIFICATION. *"For thine is the kingdom, etc."*

1. To use the Lord's prayer as a mere form is nothing better than mockery.

2. To pray the Lord's prayer sincerely, requires utmost devotion.

3. Prayer is a privilege too sacred to be trifled with.

"PREACH THE WORD"

by

Rev. Frederick Rader

ECONOMY PRINTING CONCERN

* * * * *

THE STRAIT GATE

> Strive to enter in at the strait gate; for many, I say unto you, will seek to enter in, but shall not be able (Luke 13:24).

I. THE GATE WHICH IT IS MOST DESIRABLE TO ENTER.

1. Because it is the gate of the City of Refuge.
2. Because it is the gate of a home.
3. Because it leads to a blessed feast.
4. Because the loss of those outside the gate is so terrible.

II. THERE IS A CROWD OF PEOPLE WHO WILL SEEK TO ENTER IN AND WILL NOT BE ABLE.

There is a difference between seeking and striving.

1. Some are unable to enter in because the pride of life will not let them.
2. Some are unable to enter because they seek to take sin with them.
3. Some are unable to enter because they want to postpone the matter until tomorrow.
4. Some think they are in and have mistaken the outside for the inside.

Many will seek in vain dying, and so it would appear even after death.

THREE HUNDRED OUTLINES OF SERMONS
ON THE NEW TESTAMENT
JENNINGS & GRAHAM

* * * * *

SEVEN SUBJECTS FROM THE PARABLE OF THE LOST SON

Luke 15:11-32

I. WHY GOD ALLOWS MEN TO SIN.
He divided unto him his living.

II. How and Why Men Get Away From God.
He . . . took his journey into a far country.

III. Wasted Substance, or What Satan Gives in Trade.
He wasted his substance with riotous living.

IV. Unexpected Entanglements and Consequences of Sin.
He joined himself to a citizen of that country, and he sent him . . . to feed swine.

V. The Insanity of Sin.
When he came to himself.

VI. The Place and Power of Human Decision.
I will arise and go to my father.

VII. Home, Sweet Home, or the Way Back to the Father's House.
And he arose and came to his father.

SERMON NOTES FROM THE MINISTRY OF JESUS
by
Mattie M. Boteler
The Standard Publishing Company

* * * * *

THE TEARS OF JESUS
Luke 19:41-44

Introduction: Thwarting him who has all power in heaven and on earth.

I. Jesus Mourned Over the Blindness of the People.
1. Blindness prevented them from recognizing Him.
2. It led them to attribute His mighty works to the powers of evil.
3. It hardened their hearts.

II. Jesus Mourned Over the Ingratitude of the People.

III. He Wept Over the Impending Ruin of the City.

IV. The Vision of Human Need; Weeping Over People.

V. His Love Not Abated.

SERMON NOTES FROM THE MINISTRY OF JESUS
by
Mattie M. Boteler
The Standard Publishing Company

*   *   *   *   *

CROSS OF CHRIST
Luke 23: 33, 46

I. The Cross as a Place of Emptiness (Phil. 2:7).

II. The Cross as a Place of Intercession (v. 34).
Father forgive (v. 34).

III. The Cross a Place of Shame (Heb. 12:3).

IV. The Cross a Place of Seeming Defeat (v. 35).
Obedience held Him (Phil. 2:8).
Love held Him (Gal. 2:20).
Joy held Him (Heb. 12:2).

V. The Cross a Place of Self-sacrifice (vv. 37, 39).

VI. The Cross a Place of Silence.

VII. The Cross a Place of Mercy.
Superscription in three languages: proclamation to *all* classes and conditions.

VIII. The Cross a Place of Power (v. 34).

IX. The Cross a Place of Promise (v. 43).

X. THE CROSS A PLACE OF ATONEMENT (v. 45).

XI. THE CROSS A PLACE OF JUSTICE (v. 46).

THE SEED BASKET FOR PREACHERS AND TEACHERS
FRANK J. BOYER, PUBLISHER

* * * * *

SEALED BY GOD

For him hath God the Father sealed (John 6:27).

The seal is the mark of authentication. The book of Esther often refers to the importance of the royal seal as giving validity and authenticity to documents to which it was appended. So at the waters of Jordan, God authenticated our Lord; first by the voice that spake from heaven, and secondly by the holy anointing that came upon His head, setting Him apart for holy service. "He which stablisheth us with you in Christ, and hath anointed us, is God; who hath also sealed us." In other words, God waits to authenticate us to ourselves and to the world, as His beloved children, in whom He is well pleased.

I. THE CONDITIONS OF SEALING.

In the case of our Lord there was entire subjection to the Father's will, although it involved His leaving the blessed home of Nazareth and identifying Himself with the sins and the sorrows of men, by baptism in waters where they had confessed their sins. We, too, must be prepared to obey utterly, even to death.

II. THE AGENT OF SEALING.

The Spirit descended and abode upon Him; He was filled with the Spirit, and returned in His power to Galilee. We, too, are sealed by the Holy Spirit of promise, who stamps us with the die of our Savior's image and superscription.

Simultaneously with His gracious work upon us, we may detect His loving voice within us, witnessing with our spirits that we are children of God.

III. THE EFFECT OF SEALING

Secrecy, safety and assurance (secrecy, Song of Sol. 4:12; safety, Matt. 27:65, 66; assurance, Rom. 8:15, 16, 17). There is also a daily assimilation, though we know it not, to the glorious likeness of our Lord, so that those who see us bear witness that His Name is on us.

OUR DAILY HOMILY
by
F.B. MEYER

* * * * *

IN NO WISE

He that cometh unto Me I will in no wise cast out
(John 6: 37).

Jesus was preaching from a little boat on the lake. All sorts of people were before. He invited every one to accept salvation. The invitation was extended:

I. TO THE MURDERER.

David was an example. His was the sin of adultery, murder, presumption; secret, wilful, deliberate, daring, persistent sin. "Have mercy upon me, O God, according to thy loving kindness," he prayed, and he was "saved from all his troubles."

II. TO THE MEANEST AND THE MOST SORDID.

Yes, even if fear moves them. "Why will ye die?" The prodigal thought of two things as he sat musing among the swine:

1. Of his poverty.
2. Of his father's wealth.

He finally sat a welcome guest at his father's table.

III.   To the Old in Impenitence and Habitual Sin.

The heart runs back along the years, twenty, forty, sixty years. It is hard; ears are dull, conscience is seared. But the promise! "He is able to save to the uttermost all them that come unto God by him." To the *uttermost?* Yes, to the *uttermost.* Example? The thief on the cross.

IV.   To the Burdened With Doubt.

Were ever such received? Many. Doubting Thomas. Thomas cried, "My Lord and my God."

V.   To the Backslider.

A star does not swing out of its orbit because gravitation holds it there. A sinner converted is held by the power of God, and he will be brought back from his wanderings. "Return unto me and I will have mercy upon you." A man grows cold hearted, neglects duty, forgets to pray, and still God's "Return" pursues him. Peter's backsliding was forgiven, and on the shore of the lake his commission was restored to him.

It is not for man to limit God's willingness to save, since He says, "The blood of Jesus Christ cleanseth from *all* sin."

But the invitation? It hinges on the coming of the sinner to Christ; and, next, on the sinner's trust in Jesus. "He that believeth shall be saved."

And when shall the sinner come? That question was answered by Charlotte Elliot when she wrote:

> "Just as I am—without one plea,
> But that Thy blood was shed for me,
> And that Thou bid'st me come to Thee;
> O Lamb of God, I come, I come"—

Now! Now!

A QUIVER OF ARROWS
by David James Burrell and arranged by Thomas Douglas
FUNK & WAGNALLS COMPANY

* * * * *

THE DOOR

I am the door: by Me if any man enter in, he shall be saved, and shall go in and out, and find pasture (John 10:9).

Our Lord sets Himself forth very condescendingly.

The most sublime and poetical figures are none too glorious to describe Him; but He chooses homely ones, which the most prosaic minds can apprehend.

A door is a common object. Jesus would have us often think of Him.

A door to a sheepfold is the poorest form of door. Jesus condescends to be anything, so that He may serve and save His people.

I. THE DOOR. IN THIS HOMELY ILLUSTRATION WE SEE—
   1. Necessity. Suppose there had been none, we could never have entered in to God, peace, truth, salvation, purity, or heaven.
   2. Singularity. There is only one door; let us not weary ourselves to find another. Salvation is by entrance at that door, and at none other. (Acts 4:12).

3. Personality. The Lord Jesus is Himself the door. "I am the door," saith He; not ceremonies, doctrines, professions, achievements, but the Lord Himself, our Sacrifice.

II. THE USERS OF IT.

1. They are not mere observers, or knockers at the door, or sitters down before it, or guards marching to and fro in front of it. But they *enter in* by faith, love, experience, communion.

2. They are persons who have the one qualification: they do *"enter in."* The person is "any man," but the essential distinction is entrance.

   A door which is conspicuously marked as THE DOOR is evidently meant to be used. The remarkable advertisement of "I am the door," and the special promises appended to it, are the most liberal invitation imaginable.

III. THE PRIVILEGES OF THESE USERS.

1. Salvation. "He shall be saved." At once, forever, altogether.

2. Liberty. He "shall go in and out." This is no prison-door, but a door for a flock whose Shepherd gives freedom.

3. Access. "Shall go in," for pleading, hiding, fellowship, instruction, enjoyment.

4. Egress. "He shall go out," for service, progress, etc.

5. Nourishment. "And find pasture." Our spiritual

food is found through Christ, in Christ, and around Christ.

C. H. SPURGEON'S SERMON NOTES
Edited and Condensed by David Otis Fuller
ZONDERVAN PUBLISHING HOUSE

* * * * *

THE GOOD SHEPHERD

I am the good Shepherd, and know my sheep, and am known of mine (John 10:14).

I. THE PASTORAL CHARACTER OF CHRIST.
1. He has purchased the flock.
2. He guides the flock.
3. He feeds the flock.
4. He defends the flock.

II. HIS KNOWLEDGE OF HIS PEOPLE.
1. An individual knowledge.
2. A knowledge by sympathy.

III. THEIR KNOWLEDGE OF HIM.
1. An instinct—*Spontaneity.*
2. A personal recognition.
3. An assurance.

PULPIT GERMS
by
Rev. W. W. Wythe
J. B. LIPPINCOTT COMPANY

* * * * *

BROUGHT BACK FROM THE SHADOWS
John 11:1-46

Introduction: An awe-inspiring scene.

I. WHY LAZARUS WAS BROUGHT FROM DEATH TO LIFE.
1. Not because he could not be spared from the world's work.

2. Not for the sake of his loved ones.

3. Not because death is a calamity.

4. The miracle was wrought for the glorification of God's name.

II. THE DELAY.

1. Not a sign that he did not care.

2. His purpose broader than their conceptions:
   (a) The faith of the people was confirmed.
   (b) We ourselves are richer in faith.

III. IN THE HOUSE OF MOURNING.

1. He did not make light of sorrow.

2. He wept with the heavy-hearted.

3. He gave consoling promises.

4. Lazarus lived to die again. To us is the promise that, though we die, we shall live again.

SERMON NOTES FROM THE MINISTRY OF JESUS
by
Mattie M. Boteler
THE STANDARD PUBLISHING COMPANY

* * * * *

WITNESSING
Acts 1:8

"Ye shall be witnesses unto Me"; and for this there are five essential qualifications—

I. PERSONAL KNOWLEDGE OF CHRIST.

It is essential that a witness has personal experience and knowledge of the facts to which he testifies.

II. PERSONAL CONSISTENCY.

There is a life to live as well as a story to tell. The witness of the life is most powerful.

III. PERSONAL COURAGE.

Real courage is required to speak the truth under all circumstances.

IV. PERSONAL PATIENCE.

Patience is a grace for which special grace is given.

V. PERSONAL POWER.

Divine equipment, the clothing of the individual by the Holy Spirit.

THE OUTLINED ACTS
by
Robert Lee
PICKERING & INGLIS

*   *   *   *   *

THE SUBJECT OF ISAIAH 53

He began at the same Scripture, and preached unto him Jesus (Acts 8:35).

I. THE SENSITIVE ONE.
A tender plant—verse 2.

II. THE SORROWING ONE.
A Man of Sorrows—verse 3.

III. THE SMITTEN ONE.
Smitten of God—verse 4.

IV. THE SUFFERING ONE.
He was wounded—verse 5.

V. THE SIN-BEARING ONE.
The Lord hath laid on Him—verse 6.

VI. THE SILENT ONE.
He opened not His mouth—verse 7.

VII. THE STRICKEN ONE.
The stroke was upon Him—verse 8.

VIII. THE SINCERE ONE.
No deceit in His mouth—verse 9.

IX. THE SUBMISSIVE ONE.
It pleased the Lord—verse 10.

X. THE SATISFIED ONE.
He shall be satisfied—verse 11.

XI. THE SUCCESSFUL ONE.
He shall divide the spoil—verse 12.

ONE THOUSAND SUBJECTS FOR SPEAKERS AND STUDENTS
Edited by Hy. Pickering
PICKERING & INGLIS LTD.

*   *   *   *   *

ALMOST AND ALTOGETHER

Almost thou persuadest me to be a Christian (Acts 26:28).

I. WHAT IS IT TO BE ALMOST A CHRISTIAN?

1. Mere knowledge of the way of salvation through Christ.

2. Mere conviction of the desirableness of embracing Him.

3. Mere excitement concerning our relation to Him.

4. Mere reformation of our outward lives.

II. WHAT IS IT TO BE ALTOGETHER A CHRISTIAN?
1. To believe in Christ's doctrines.
2. To rely on His atonement.
3. To love His person.
4. To practice His religion.

PULPIT GERMS
by
Rev. W. W. Wythe
J. B. LIPPINCOTT COMPANY

*   *   *   *   *

PAUL'S VOYAGE AND SHIPWRECK

Acts 27

I. DIVINE PROTECTION.

Julius, although a Roman centurion, is kindly disposed toward Paul, and brings him safely to Rome. God was at the back of the arrangement—verse 1.

II. PERILOUS REJECTION.

Paul's wise advice to the mariners was rejected; like the Gospel today—verses 10, 11.

III. PREVAILING INTERCESSION.

During the great storm Paul had been praying for the safety of the 275 lives on board—verses 21, 22.

IV. COMPLETE SALVATION.

All lives saved—verse 22.

V. PERSONAL DEVOTION.

Whose I am—possession; whom I serve—consecration —verse 23.

VI. PERFECT RESIGNATION.

The storm was unabated. He did not trust the ship, for it was doomed; nor the sailors, a bad lot; but against all appearances he trusted God—verse 25.

ONE THOUSAND SUBJECTS FOR SPEAKERS AND STUDENTS
Collected by Hy. Pickering
PICKERING & INGLIS LTD.

* * * * *

SEVEN BLESSINGS IN ROMANS 5

I. PEACE.

We have peace with God—verse 1.

II. PLACE.

Access by faith . . . wherein we stand—verse 2.

III. PROSPECT.
Rejoice in hope of the glory of God—verse 2.

IV. POWER.
Love of God shed abroad . . . Holy Ghost—verse 5.

V. PRIEST.
We shall be saved by His life—verse 10.

VI. PORTION.
We joy in God—verse 11.

VII. PERSON.
Through our Lord Jesus Christ—verse 12.

TWELVE BASKETS FULL OF ORIGINAL OUTLINES
AND SCRIPTURE STUDIES
Compiled by Hy. Pickering
PICKERING & INGLIS LTD.

* * * * *

PEACE WITH GOD
Rom. 5:1

I. IN THE AFFECTIONS.

II. IN THE WILL.

III. IN THE CONSCIENCE.

We have peace with God, because the bad past is blotted out.

We have peace with God because, being justified, we are no longer condemned.

We have peace with God because our warfare against God ceases and friendship is begun.

We have peace with God because of His smile and approval.

THE SEED BASKET FOR PREACHERS AND TEACHERS
FRANK J. BOYER, PUBLISHER

* * * * *

THE NEW LIFE
Romans 8 : 12-14

I. THIS IS A LIFE NOT AFTER THE FLESH.

"We are debtors not to live after the flesh." Fleshly wisdom or energy could never produce such a life. It is a life which ye have from God. Born of God.

II. THIS LIFE OWES NOTHING TO THE FLESH.

"We are debtors *not to the flesh.*" It received nothing from the flesh, gave nothing to it. The new man owes the old man nothing. Let the time past suffice for the will of the flesh.

III. THIS IS A LIFE OPPOSED TO THE FLESH.

"Mortify the deeds of the body." The salvation brought to us by the grace of God teaches us to deny *all* ungodliness. Paul kept his body under lest he should be cast aside as a useless weapon (I Cor. 9:2-7).

IV. THIS LIFE SHOULD BE IN THE POWER OF THE SPIRIT.

"If ye *through* the Spirit." In yielding to the Spirit we shall obey the truth, thereby our souls shall be purified (I Peter 1:22). This is God's great purpose concerning us (II Thess. 2:13).

V. THIS LIFE IS TO BE UNDER THE CONTROL OF THE SPIRIT.

"Led by the Spirit." When the Spirit comes within us it is that we might "walk in His ways" (Ezek. 36:27). He will guide you into all truth.

VI. THIS IS TO BE A LIFE OF FELLOWSHIP.

"Sons of God." Beloved now are we the sons of God. Our fellowship is with the Father, and with His Son Jesus Christ, and in the *Communion* of the Holy Ghost.

HANDFULS ON PURPOSE
Series IX
by
Pastor James Smith
PICKERING & INGLIS LTD.

*   *   *   *   *

THE CHRISTIAN'S INSURANCE POLICY

And we know that all things work together for good to them that love God, to them who are the called according to his purpose (Rom. 8 : 28).

Consider the working of God's providence. God works:

I. UNIVERSALLY. "All things."

1. All provisions of nature are destined for our good.
2. So also, all the provisions of grace—Sabbath, Scriptures, Sanctuary, etc.

II. ENERGETICALLY. "Work."

Work, here used to denote the most intense, tireless activity.

III. HARMONIOUSLY. "Together."

1. Worlds work together—world balances world.
2. Men work together with men, with angels, and with God.

IV. BENEFICENTLY. "For good."

Good here does not necessarily apply to our health, ease or fortune—but to our eternal interest. *Good* looks to heaven and points to eternity—II Cor. 4 :7.

1. The trials of those who are called to bear the cross for Christ's sake.
2. The ordinary calamities which we may be called to suffer.

V. Specifically. "To them."

  1. To them that love God; this love must be:
    (a) Paramount.
    (b) Practical—a ruling, practical force.
    (c) Permanent—in everything and forever.

  2. To them that are the called according to His purpose.

VI. Assuredly. "We know."

It is not a mere conjecture, an opinion; it is a declaration of absolute certainty; we have the promise of God that cannot lie, and the power of God that cannot fail.

  1. We know it by revelation.

    We know it by reason.

  3. We know it by experience.

  4. The assurance is in perfect harmony with God's Word.

  5. With the experience of God's people; e.g. Moses, Joseph.

How blessed and glorious to be a child of God and know that "all things work together."

"PREACH THE WORD"
by
Rev. Frederick Rader
Economy Printing Concern

*   *   *   *   *

SPIRITUAL TRANSFORMATION

Predestined to be conformed to the image of His Son
(Romans 8:29).

I. How the Image is Produced.

  1. Moulding—in clay. (Jer. 18:2, 6; Isa. 64:8; 45:9). "Lie still and let Him mould thee."—*Luther.*

  2. Sealing—in wax or clay. (Job 38:14; II Tim. 2:19).

  3. Reflecting—in a mirror. (II Cor. 3:18; Prov. 27:19).

4. Engraving—in precious stones. (Ex. 28:9-21).

5. Writing on tablets. (II Cor. 3:3).

6. Stamping or casting—metals. (Mark 12:16; II Chron. 4:17).

7. Carving—in wood. (I Kings 6:18; Ex. 31:5).

II. WHAT PREPARATION IS NEEDED.

1. The clay—dug up. (Isa. 57:1).

2. The wax—melted. (Ps. 22:14; Ps. 97:5).

3. The mirror—polished.
"If the polish of the mirror were perfect, it would be invisible; we should simply see the image of what is reflected."—*Prof. Tyndall on "Reflection."*

4. The stones—hewn. (Isa. 51:1; I Kings 5:17). Polished (Ps. 144:12).

5. The precious stones—found. (Job 28:6). Prepared, (I Chron. 29:2). Cut and set (Ex. 31:5).

6. The metals—sought (Prov. 2:4; Job 28:1, 2). Dug up (Job 28:2). Melted (Prov. 17:3). Purified (Mal. 3:3; Prov. 25:4).

7. The wood—hewn. (I Kings 5:6). "Is not this the carpenter?" (Mark 6:3).

NOTES FROM MY BIBLE
by D. L. Moody
BIBLE INSTITUTE COLPORTAGE ASS'N

* * * * *

THE CHRISTIAN REVELATION
I Corinthians 2:9-16

I. THIS REVELATION CANNOT POSSIBLY BE THE INVENTION OF MEN.

The *eye* of man's carnal mind hath never seen it. The *ear* of man's worldly wisdom hath never heard it. Neither hath it ever entered into the heart of man (apart from the Holy Spirit) the things which God hath prepared for them that *love Him* (v. 9), and since the *beginning of the world* it hath been so (Isa. 64:4). The world by wisdom knew not God (chap. 1:21).

II. IT IS A REVELATION FROM GOD.

"But God hath revealed them unto us" (v. 10). God only could reveal the mysteries of His suffering Son. "O the depths of the riches, both of the wisdom and knowledge of God concerning His Son" (Rom. 11:33). This is the glory of the Gospel message, that it is as true and as gracious as the God who gave it (Gal. 1:12).

III. WHAT THIS REVELATION IS.

It is the unveiling of the mystery of Christ and Him crucified (v. 2). The revelation of the fact that He died *for our sins,* and rose again *for our justification,* and that He is coming again for our final deliverance (Heb. 9:26). It is a revelation of His abounding grace to sinful men, and of His power to save to the very uttermost all that come unto Him.

IV. HOW THIS REVELATION IS MADE KNOWN.

"God hath revealed them unto us *by His Spirit*" (v. 10). It has come from God, and it comes home to the believing heart by the Spirit of God. For "the Spirit searcheth the deep things of God." "The things of God no man knoweth without the Spirit of God" (v. 11). The Holy Spirit is the minister of the things of Christ (I Cor. 12:8-11). He is the "Spirit of Truth," and He shall teach you all things bearing on the revealed will of the Father, "for He shall receive of Mine and shall shew it unto you" (John 16:13).

V. HOW THESE THINGS SHOULD BE PREACHED.

"My preaching was not with enticing words of man's wisdom, but in demonstration of the Spirit and of power"

(v. 4). "Our Gospel came not unto you in word only, but also in power and in the Holy Ghost" (I Thess. 1:5). Without this power, preaching is without authority—"sounding brass." There may be a demonstration of eloquent words and fleshly energy, but without the demonstration of the Spirit it is spiritually powerless (v. 13).

VI. The Christian's Attitude Towards This Divine Revelation.

"I am determined not to know anything among you, save Jesus Christ and Him crucified" (v. 2). In Corinth there were many contentions, as there are in the world everywhere today. But Paul knew that the one thing needed by all was the power of the Gospel of Christ. The worldly, in their wisdom, would call this narrow-minded; but it is the wisdom of God to offer the Divine remedy for all the world's woes.

HANDFULS ON PURPOSE
Series X
by Pastor James Smith
Pickering & Inglis Ltd.

* * * * *

THE CHRISTIAN RACE

Know ye not that they which run in a race run all, but one receiveth the prize? So run that ye may obtain (I Cor. 9:24).

I. The Race.
  1. Its necessity.
  2. Its rules.

II. The Runner.
  1. Simplicity of aim.
  2. Earnestness of spirit.
  3. Perseverance to the end.

III. THE PRIZE.
   1. For all competitors.
   2. Incorruptible.

PULPIT GERMS
by
Rev. W. W. Wythe
J. B. LIPPINCOTT COMPANY

*   *   *   *   *

STEADFASTNESS

Therefore, my beloved brethren, be ye steadfast, un-moveable, always abounding in the work of the Lord, for-asmuch as ye know that your labor is not in vain in the Lord (I Cor. 15:58).

I. AN ARGUMENTATION. "Therefore."
   1. Because Christ is risen.
   2. Believers shall rise.
   3. Death is defeated.
   4. Victory is sure.

II. AN IDENTIFICATION. "Beloved."
The text is not addressed to the backslider, the false professor, much less to the mere formalist, the sinner—but to the brethren, beloved of God. God's own.

III. AN EXHORTATION. "Be ye steadfast."
   1. To unmovable steadfastness:—
      (a) In doctrine—all the great doctrines of the Bible; know what you know.
      (b) In experience—try the spirits—prove all things—taste and see.
      (c) In practice.
   2. To abounding work.
      (a) The various spheres for works:—

Our own hearts and lives.
Our own homes and families.
Our own Sunday School.
Our own prayer meeting.
Our own church.
Our own world.

(b) The measure—abundant, much work, more work.

(c) The time—always, not Sundays only, or fair weather or revivals.

IV. An Occupation. "Work of the Lord."

1. Think of the preparation for this work; four thousand years of priests, seers, miracles as preliminary.

2. Of the sacrifices made; the incarnate God lived, suffered and died.

3. Of the unceasing agency of the Holy Spirit in order to effect it.

4. Of its wonderful results; millions of lost souls redeemed to the knowledge, image, fellowship and service of God.

V. A Remuneration.

1. Here in this life—thirty, sixty and even a hundredfold; peace of mind—conscience.

2. Hereafter in the life to come—victory over sin, death and the grave. Everlasting life, joy, peace, pleasure.

The great need of the hour is men; men of courage, fidelity, prayer; men for whom no night is too dark, no road too long, no opposition too great.

"PREACH THE WORD"
by
Rev. Frederick Rader
Economy Printing Concern

* * * * *

THE GLORY REVEALED IN US

For God, who commanded the light to shine out of darkness, hath shined in our hearts, to give the light of the knowledge of the glory of God in the face of Jesus Christ (II Cor. 4:6).

I. THE AUTHOR OF SPIRITUAL ILLUMINATION.
   1. God the Creator.
   2. In the exercise of creating power.

II. THE SPHERE OF SPIRITUAL ILLUMINATION.
   1. The human heart.
   2. Through the medium of the understanding.
   3. By the instrumentality of the word.

III. THE MEDIUM OF SPIRITUAL ILLUMINATION.
   1. Jesus Christ the only manifestation of God's glory.
   2. Jesus Christ the complete exhibition of God's glory.

PULPIT GERMS
by
Rev. W. W. Wythe
J. B. LIPPINCOTT COMPANY

* * * * *

THE DEVELOPMENT OF THE SPIRIT IN GALATIANS

   I. THE SPIRIT PROMISED—chap. 3:14.
  II. THE SPIRIT SENT FORTH—chap. 4:6.
 III. THE SPIRIT MINISTERED—chap. 3:5.
  IV. THE SPIRIT RECEIVED—chap. 3:2.
   V. A BEGINNING MADE IN THE SPIRIT—chap. 3:3.
  VI. LIVING IN THE SPIRIT—chap. 5:25.
 VII. LED BY THE SPIRIT—chap. 5:18.
VIII. THE WARRING OF THE SPIRIT—chap. 5:17.
  IX. SOWING TO THE SPIRIT—chap. 6:8.

X.   FRUIT OF THE SPIRIT—chap. 5:22.

XI. WAITING FOR THE HOPE OF RIGHTEOUSNESS THROUGH THE SPIRIT—chap. 5:5.

TWELVE BASKETS FULL OF ORIGINAL OUTLINES
AND SCRIPTURE STUDIES
Compiled by Hy. Pickering
PICKERING & INGLIS LTD.

*   *   *   *   *

"WHO GAVE HIMSELF FOR ME"
Galatians 2:20

I.   GAVE HIS HEAD TO WEAR THE THORNS FOR ME—John 19:2.

II.   GAVE HIS EYES TO WEEP TEARS FOR ME—Luke 19:41.

III. GAVE HIS CHEEK TO BE SMITTEN FOR ME—Lam. 3:30.

IV.   GAVE HIS TONGUE TO PRAY FOR ME—Luke 23:34.

V.   GAVE HIS SHOULDERS TO BEAR THE BURDEN FOR ME—Luke 15:5.

VI.   GAVE HIS BACK TO BE PLOUGHED FOR ME—Psa. 129:3.

VII. GAVE HIS SIDE TO THE SPEAR FOR ME—John 19:34.

VIII. GAVE HIS HAND TO THE NAILS FOR ME—Psa. 22:16.

IX.   GAVE HIS FEET TO THE IRON SPIKES FOR ME—Psa. 22:16.

X.   GAVE HIS PRECIOUS, PRECIOUS BLOOD FOR ME—Acts 20:28.

XI.   GAVE HIS SOUL AN OFFERING FOR ME—Isa. 53:12.

XII. GAVE HIS LIFE FOR ME—John 10:11.

XIII. GAVE ALL HIS RICHES AND BECAME POOR FOR ME—II Cor. 8:9.

XIV. WILL NEVER REST TILL HE COMES AGAIN FOR ME
—John 14:3.

TWELVE BASKETS FULL OF ORIGINAL OUTLINES
AND SCRIPTURE STUDIES
Compiled by Hy. Pickering
PICKERING & INGLIS LTD.

* * * * *

THE FRUIT OF THE SPIRIT

But the fruit of the Spirit is love, joy, peace, long-
suffering, gentleness, goodness, faith, meekness, temperance
(Gal. 5:22, 23).

We have "the works of the flesh," but we do not read of
"the fruits of the Spirit," but in the singular number—fruit.

The nine graces are one fruit.

I. ALL THE OTHER FRUITS OF THE SPIRIT ARE ONLY THE
EXPANSION OF THE FIRST.

Joy is love triumphing; peace is love resting; long-suffer-
ing is love under the great, and gentleness is love under
the little trials of life; goodness is love going forth into
action; faith is love sitting and receiving back again to its
own bosom; meekness is love controlling the passions of
the mind; temperance, the same love subduing the passions
of the body. The law of the Spirit is all contained in one
word, and the unity of the whole Christian character is
"love." Fruit is not fruit if it is not sweet. What is anything to God till there is love in it? Therefore love stands
first.

II. THERE IS A LAW OF GROWTH ABOUT THE SPIRIT OF
GOD IN MAN.

This is as sure as the law which regulates the growth and
development of any plant. This truth is wrapped up in
the metaphor "the fruit of the Spirit." If there is not

advance in the image of Christ, it is because the work of the Holy Ghost is obstructed, for the Spirit, in Himself, always essentially grows.

III. To be Fruit-bearers We Must be Engrafted Into the True Vine.

If there is one state more solemn than another it is the leafy state. What if Jesus, drawing nigh to any one of us and finding nothing but leaves, should punish the barrenness which is wilful by the barrenness which is judicial: "No man eat fruit of thee hereafter for ever."

THREE HUNDRED OUTLINES OF SERMONS
ON THE NEW TESTAMENT
Jennings & Graham

* * * * *

RICHES OF GRACE
Eph. 1:7

I. Foreknown (Rom. 8:29; I Pet. 1:2; Eph. 1:4).

II. Predestinated (Rom. 8:30; Eph. 1:11).

III. Called (Rom. 8:30; 9:23, 24; I Pet. 5:10).

IV. Justified (Rom. 8:30; Titus 3:7).

V. Glorified (Rom. 8:30; Eph. 2:6; I John 3:2).

VI. Made One With Himself (Col. 1:18; Eph. 5:23). Partakers of the Divine Nature (II Pet. 1:4; Heb. 2:11).

VII. Blessed in Him With All Spiritual Blessings (Eph. 2:4; Jno. 1:16).

"Who shall separate us?" (Rom. 8:35). "I am persuaded that neither life, nor death, nor any other creature" (Rom. 8:38, 39).

How safe, how satisfied, the souls that cling to Him!

TWELVE BASKETS FULL OF ORIGINAL OUTLINES
AND SCRIPTURE STUDIES
Compiled by Hy. Pickering
PICKERING & INGLIS LTD.

*   *   *   *   *

THE SINNER'S STATE BY NATURE
As described in Ephesians 2:12

   I.   CHRISTLESS—"Without Christ."

  II.   FRIENDLESS—"Aliens."

III.   HOMELESS—"Strangers."

 IV.   HOPELESS—"Having no Hope."

  V.   GODLESS—"Without God."

FIVE HUNDRED SCRIPTURE OUTLINES
by
John Ritchie
JOHN RITCHIE, PUBLISHER

*   *   *   *   *

THE ATTITUDE OF THE CHRISTIAN WARRIOR
Having done all, to stand (Eph. 6:13).

The text may refer to the end of the strife, "having overcome all," or to the equipment of the soldier and the fulfillment of regular duty.

I. STAND READY.

   1. Conflict must be expected.

   2. The assaults of the enemy may be sudden and unforeseen.

   3. Therefore, "put on the whole armour of God."

II. STAND STEADY.

   1. Our stability will be tested.

2. Firmness in temptation and adversity is a great achievement.

III. STAND VICTORIOUS.

1. This will happen again and again through life.

2. The final victory will be glorious.

SEEDS AND SAPLINGS
by
F. J. AUSTIN

*   *   *   *   *

HEAVENLY SHOES

And your feet shod with the preparation of the gospel of peace (Eph. 6:15).

I. LET US EXAMINE THE SHOES.

1. They come from the blessed Maker. One Who is skillful in all arts, and knows by experience what is wanted, since He has Himself journeyed through life's roughest ways.

2. They are made of excellent material: "the preparation of the gospel of peace." Well seasoned, soft in wear, lasting long.
Peace with God as to the past, the future, the present.
Peace with the Word and all its teachings.
Peace with one's inner self, conscience, fears, desires, etc.

3. They are such shoes as Jesus wore, and all the saints.

4. They are such as will never wear out: they are old, yet ever new; we may wear them at all ages and in all places.

II. LET US TRY THEM ON.

Observe with delight—

1. Their perfect fitness. They are made to suit each one of us.

2. Their excellent foothold: we can tread with holy boldness upon our high places with these shoes.

3. Their marching powers for daily duty. No one grows weary or footsore when he is thus shod.

4. Their wonderful protection against trials by the way. "Thou shalt tread on the lion and adder" (Ps. 91:13).

III. LET US LOOK AT THE BAREFOOTED AROUND US.

The sinner is unshod. Yet he kicks against the pricks. How can he hope to fulfill the heavenly pilgrimage?

The professor is slipshod, or else he wears tight shoes. His fine slippers will soon be worn out. He loves not the gospel, knows not its peace, seeks not its preparation.

The gospel alone supplies a fit shoe for all feet. To the gospel let us fly at once. Come, poor shoeless beggar!

C. H. SPURGEON'S SERMON NOTES
Edited and Condensed by David Otis Fuller
ZONDERVAN PUBLISHING HOUSE

* * * * *

SAINTS IN CAESAR'S HOUSEHOLD
Philippians 4:22

INTRODUCTION.

1. Paul is sending a letter to the Church in Philippi.

2. He sits in all the rude discomforts of an Eastern prison, writing amidst much difficulty, secured by a coupling chain to a soldier.

3. Here are his closing words.

I. THEIR NAME.

The New Testament has several names for believers, each of which expresses some great truth.

1. *Believers* (Acts 5:14; I Tim. 4:12). The central bond which bound them. Bond of faith.

2. *Brethren* (Matt. 12:48; Matt. 23:8; Matt. 28:10).
   (a) This is a name by which they were known.
   (b) It spoke of their common relation to a Father.
   (c) And pledged them to the sweetness and blessedness of a family.

3. *Christians* (Acts 11:26). The sarcastic wits of Antioch called them Christians. Name suggesting not only adherents of some founder of a school or party, but followers of Christ.

4. *Disciples* (Matt. 27:57).
   (a) Their humble attitude of learning.
   (b) Their Lord's authority acknowledged.

5. *Saint* (I Cor. 1:2).
   (a) A prophecy of personal character.
   (b) What God expects us to be.

II. THEIR ABODE.

1. Who was this Caesar? Nero, a monster of iniquity, a man who has been described as "half beast and half devil." He was a clown, a sensualist, and a murderer.

2. His presence had poisoned the very atmosphere of the Imperial Palace, making it a sty of filth.

3. And yet there were shining saints living there day by day.

III. THEIR DANGER.

1. *Moral.*
   (a) A strange place to find saints.

(b) Let no man say it is impossible to live a pure life in any circumstance.

2. *Spiritual.* It was a materialistic atmosphere.
3. *Physical.*
   (a) Life was cheap.
   (b) On the least pretext people were executed.

IV. OUR DANGER.

1. Our Nero has changed.
2. It is not a persecuting world that is now our greatest foe, but a tempting world.
3. To stand against the sword of the world is difficult. To stand against its sneers is more so. But to stand against its allurements is more difficult still.

HANDFULS ON PURPOSE
Series XII
by Robert Lee
PICKERING & INGLIS LTD.

* * * * *

THE FAITHFUL SAYING

This is a faithful saying, and worthy of all acceptation, that Christ Jesus came into the world to save sinners: of whom I am chief (I Tim. 1:15).

Paul had described his ordination in verse 12. He then went on to speak of the grace manifested in the call of such a person to the ministry (verse 13), and of the further grace by which he was sustained in that ministry.

I. HOW WE PREACH THE GOSPEL.

1. As a certainty. It is a "faithful saying." *We* do not doubt the truth of our message, or how could we expect *you* to believe it. We believe, and are sure, because

It is a revelation of God.

It is attested by miracles.

It bears its witness within itself.

It has proved its power upon our hearts.

2. As an everyday truth. It is to us a "saying" or proverb.

3. As claiming your attention. "Worthy of all acceptation."

You must believe it to be true.

You must appropriate it to yourself.

You ought to do so, for it is worthy of your acceptance.

II. What Gospel Do We Preach?

1. The gospel of a person: "Christ Jesus."

He is the anointed of God: "Christ."

He is the Saviour of men: "Jesus."

He is God and Man in One Person.

He died, and yet He lives forever.

2. The gospel for sinners.

For such Jesus lived and labored.

For such He died and made atonement.

For such He has sent the gospel of pardon.

For such He pleads in heaven.

3. The gospel of effectual deliverance. "To save sinners."

Not to half save them.

Nor to make them salvable.

Nor to help them to save themselves.

Nor to save them as righteous.

But to save them wholly and effectually from their sins.

III. Why Do We Preach It?

1. Because we have been saved by it.

2. Because we cannot help it, for an inward impulse compels us to tell of the miracle of mercy wrought upon us.

Will you not believe a saying so sure?

Will you not accept a truth so gladsome?

Will you not come to a Saviour so suitable?

C. H. SPURGEON'S SERMON NOTES
Edited and Condensed by David Otis Fuller
ZONDERVAN PUBLISHING HOUSE

* * * * *

A GOOD SOLDIER
II Timothy 2: 3, 4

The metaphor is very appropriate. Christ is our Captain, and we as soldiers have a real and *standing* engagement with the forces of evil without and within (Eph. 6:11-13). The qualifications of a good soldier of Jesus Christ are here indicated. He must be—

I. ACCEPTED.

"Chosen." Not every one is fit for a soldier, bodily defects may hinder; so moral and spiritual defects hinder from being a *good* soldier of Jesus Christ. It is His to choose. "Chosen of God." He hath chosen the weak things, etc.

II. SEPARATED.

"No *entangling of himself* with other affairs." It is said that when an officer who had been ordered to the Cape asked leave to stay at home, Wellington said, "Sail or sell." Everything that would hinder in the service of God must be forsaken. "Seek *first* the kingdom."

III. CONSECRATED.

"That he may *please Him.*" One is your Master. Present *yourselves* unto God (Rom. 12:1, 2).

IV. PERSEVERING.

"Endure hardness." "They persecuted Me, they will also persecute you," says the Captain. But be not discouraged because of the way.

V. SELF-EMPTIED.

"Put on the *armour of God,*" having no confidence in the flesh. Then victory is certain (I Cor. 15:57, 58). The walls of every Jericho will fall before faith.

HANDFULS ON PURPOSE
Series II
by Pastor James Smith
PICKERING & INGLIS LTD.

* * * * *

THE GREAT SALVATION

How shall we escape, if we neglect so great salvation?
(Heb. 2:3).

I. God has provided for men and offered to them the great salvation.

II. This salvation is offered to all men as the offer finds them.

III. This God-provided and God-offered salvation is by many neglected.

IV. All who neglect this great salvation, are cherishing the hope that somehow or other they will after all, escape.

V. Escape in the neglect of the Gospel salvation is an absolute impossibility. Be advised then, and listen now to the overtures of peace which God is making. Put away your indifference and accept His grace in Christ.

THREE HUNDRED OUTLINES OF SERMONS
ON THE NEW TESTAMENT
JENNINGS & GRAHAM

* * * * *

THE ANCHOR

"Which hope we have as an anchor to the soul" (Heb. 6: 17-20).

Faith is the divinely-appointed way of receiving the blessings of grace. The wonders of creation, discoveries of revelation, the movements of providence, are all intended to create and foster the principle of faith in the living God. Both the works and words of God co-operate to educate men in the grace of faith. Have faith in God, for faith is in itself a virtue of the highest order. Faith is a root from which may grow all that can adorn the human character. "The just shall live by faith"; essential to the vitality of Christianity. There is a place for the unbelieving, but it is not heaven.

I. THE DESIGN OF THE ANCHOR.

To hold firmly. God has given us certain great truths to hold our minds fast. To save wreckage, to keep a vessel from discomfort, strong consolation. To preserve us from losing the headway we have made. Sometimes saints discouraged are inclined to drift back. Down should go the anchor. Do not aspire to the charity which grows out of uncertainty. That we may possess constancy and usefulness. A feeble man easily moved by this or that will always be of feeble faith.

II. THE MAKE OF THE ANCHOR.

Anchor making is responsible work. What is our anchor? It has two great blades, each acting as a holdfast. Ours is God's promise and His oath. Find out in Scripture the many holdfasts we have.

III. OUR HOLD OF THE ANCHOR.

We must have hold. The anchor may be sure, and have a good grip, but it must be connected with a cable. Timid ones ask, May we? Yes, we are urged to grasp God's promise with a God-created confidence.

IV. THE ANCHOR'S HOLD OF US.

Hope should hold us, even in trial and affliction. Our security depends far more upon God's holding us than our holding Him. The unseen grip of the anchor; out of sight, within the veil. The more the ship drags, the tighter its hold becomes. Most solid assurance to rest upon.

To those who have no anchor: What will you do in the hour of storm?

THE PREACHER'S AND TEACHER'S VADE-MECUM
Compiled by J. Ellis
ALLENSON & CO. LIMITED

* * * * *

FOUR ASPECTS OF SALVATION
In I Peter 1: 1-5

I. ELECT by the will of the Father (verse 1).

II. SHELTERED by the Blood of the Son (verse 2).

III. BEGOTTEN by the Resurrection of Christ (verse 3).

IV. KEPT by the Power of God (verse 5).

FIVE HUNDRED SCRIPTURE OUTLINES
by
John Ritchie
JOHN RITCHIE, PUBLISHER

* * * * *

GOD'S PEOPLE
But ye are a peculiar people (I Peter 2: 9).

I. GOD'S PEOPLE ARE A PROFESSING PEOPLE.

II. GOD'S PEOPLE ARE A SEPARATED PEOPLE.

III. GOD'S PEOPLE ARE A SUFFERING PEOPLE.

IV. GOD'S PEOPLE ARE A PRAYING PEOPLE.

V.   GOD'S PEOPLE ARE A SANCTIFIED PEOPLE.
VI. GOD'S PEOPLE ARE A BLESSED PEOPLE.

PULPIT GERMS
by
Rev. W. W. Wythe
J. B. LIPPINCOTT COMPANY

*   *   *   *   *

OUR FATHER'S CARE
He careth for you (I Peter 5:7).

This is not an exhortation, but a statement of a fact which can hardly be apprehended without carrying with it a tremendous exhortation, whose urgency grows in proportion as we grow to know the fact more fully. We can hardly come to know it completely, but may approach it by looking from several points of view.

I.   GOD'S CARE PROVIDES A PLACE FOR US.

God did not make man till he had prepared a place for him, planting a garden "eastward in Eden," and filling it with fragrant flowers and all manner of pleasant fruits for his enjoyment. This was not an exceptional provision for man's early innocence alone. A place for his abode and work is an essential part of God's care, not only now, but forever. When Christ was leaving His disciples and thinking of the consummation of human life, He said, "I go to prepare a place for you."

It is not always a garden. Rasselas, "Prince of Abyssinia," in Johnson's story, was unhappy in his lovely valley. But God has a place in His ordered system for every man, and that place underlies one's work and hope.

II. GOD'S CARE IS NOT MERELY FOR THE ORDER OF HIS SYSTEM, BUT PERSONAL, WITH REGARD FOR MAN'S INDIVIDUALITY.

He says, "Behold I stand at the door and knock." He waits on our personal action, but His patient waiting is not with the cold face of an inscrutable destiny. God has all the winning and gracious ways with which a wise mother knows how to persuade her children to choose wisely. A lot of garden vines had failed to twine themselves for healthy, supported growth, and it was no little work to lift them from the ground, disentangle them from noxious weeds, and then, without breaking or bruising, to start them as they ought to grow. A gardener needs to know in what direction the vines naturally twine, and a hundred things more; and then he has to handle them with patient and persistent care.

III. GOD'S CARE IS MORE THAN RESPECT FOR MIGHT, OR EVEN FOR STRICT RIGHT.

We care for good men, and successful men; but God cares for weak men who are making a failure of their lives, to save them from failure, and help them into true success. His care for us sees our ill-desert, and forgives and redeems and restores. He cares even for "the outcasts of Israel."

IV. GOD'S CARE CONNECTS OUR LITTLE LIVES WITH THE GREAT WORLD MOVEMENT FOR RIGHT, SO GIVING TO US WORTH AND DIGNITY.

God's kingdom is made up by the union of principles and men. We see the King on His throne of righteousness. We know that in His heart are all holiness and justice and truth, and we know that we are unholy, and have often been unjust, and our truth is perverted with prejudice, and we shrink away from Him. But He reaches out His strong and tender hand, and lays hold of us in love, and draws us to His breast, and says: You are my child; come take in this holiness and justice and truth which are my nature, for what I wish is that these principles should be embodied in men. His kingdom is the incarnation of the great principles of holy love and truth.

V. HIS CARE IS NOT MERELY FOR US AS WE ARE, BUT MORE FOR US AS WE SHALL BE WITH HIS TEACHING AND HELP.

Nothing is uglier than a childish look in a face old enough to show thought and character; but there are many men whose spiritual nature is dwarfed, and we wonder whether they have read Paul's "When I became a man, I put away childish things."

We love a little child, but would be pained to think the childish beauty would never give place to manliness, even though wrinkled and sobered, if not saddened, as the years make their mark of thought and character. So God does not care so much for our present gladness, some of which is childish, as for the sober satisfaction we shall have in work and trial.

VI. CONCLUSION.

We should make much of what God does in our life; and care for the things He cares for.

Look not about you at the difficulties in your way, else you will lose courage; nor within at your failures and the weakness that brought them; but look up at Christ. So shall you face the sunny south, and fill your life with cheer.

SERMONS IN ILLUSTRATION
by Franklin Noble, D. D.
E. B. TREAT & COMPANY

* * * * *

THE LIGHT OF THE GOSPEL

The darkness is past, and the true light now shineth
(I John 2:8).

I. THE DARKNESS OF THE PAST.
  1. The darkness of heathenism.
  2. The darkness of Judaism.
  3. The darkness of a corrupt Christianity.

II. THE LIGHT OF THE PRESENT.
  1. The Bible.
  2. Preaching of the Word.
  3. Education.
  4. The press.

III. THE GLORY TO BE REVEALED.
  1. Universal progress.
  2. Universal brotherhood.
  3. Universal prevalence of Christianity.

PULPIT GERMS
by
Rev. W. W. Wythe
J. B. LIPPINCOTT COMPANY

*   *   *   *   *

BY-AND-BY

It doth not yet appear what we shall be: but we know
that when He shall appear, we shall be like Him; for we
shall see Him as He is (I John 3:2).

I. "IT DOTH NOT YET APPEAR WHAT WE SHALL BE."
At present we are veiled, and travel through the world
incognito.

  1. Our Master was not made manifest here below.
     His glory was veiled in flesh.
     His Deity was concealed in infirmity.
     His power was hidden under sorrow and weakness.

His riches were buried under poverty and shame.
The world knew Him not, for He was made flesh.

2. We must needs have an evening before our morning,
   a schooling before our college, a tuning before the
   music is ready.

3. This is not the time in which to appear in our glory.
   The winter prepares flowers, but does not call them
   forth.

   The ebb-tide reveals the secrets of the sea, but many
   of our rivers no gallant ship can then sail.

   To everything there is a season, and this is not the
   time of glory.

II. "BUT WE KNOW THAT WHEN HE SHALL APPEAR."

1. We speak of our Lord's manifestation without doubt.
   "We know."

2. Our faith is so assured that it becomes knowledge.
   He will be manifest upon this earth in person.

III. "WE SHALL BE LIKE HIM."

1. Having a body like His body.
   Sinless, incorruptible, painless, spiritual, clothed with
   beauty and power, and yet most real and true.

2. Having a soul like His soul.
   Perfect, holy, instructed, developed, strengthened,
   active, delivered from temptation, conflict, and suffering.

3. Having such dignities and glories as He wears.
   Kings, priests, conquerors, judges, sons of God.

IV. "WE SHALL SEE HIM AS HE IS."

1. This glorious sight will perfect our likeness.

2. This will be the result of our being like Him.

3. This will be evidence of our being like Him, since none but the pure in heart can see God.
   The sight will be ravishing.
   The sight will be transforming and transfiguring.
   The sight will be abiding, and a source of bliss forever.

C. H. SPURGEON'S SERMON NOTES
Edited and Condensed by David Otis Fuller
ZONDERVAN PUBLISHING HOUSE

* * * * *

LOVING ONE ANOTHER

Beloved, if God so loved us, we ought also to love one another (I John 4:11).

This word "beloved" reveals the heart of the writer. This term of endearment, and indeed all kindred terms, were either created or adopted by the spirit of the apostle. The word "if" does not express doubt as to the love of God, but carries with it the meaning of "because."

I. If God so loved us, we ought also to love one another, because ignorance of what God means by love must now be wilful. Some professing Christians ask, What is love? We answer by pointing to God giving His only-begotten Son.

II. Because doubt and uncertainty as to the objects of love are forever excluded. Our natural inclination is to love those only who love us; to salute our elect brethren and sisters only. But to elect the objects of our love selfishly and capriciously, and to limit these objects wantonly, is to transgress God's law.

III. Because the power of love to conquer obstacles and impediments is in God's case most gloriously shown.

IV. Because the restoration of love between man and man is one of God's objects in that redemption which so proves His love for us. He seeks to save us from an unloving state.

V. Because we require to be followers of God as dear children. We cannot follow God in every path, but Christ strengthening us, and the Spirit of God sanctifying us, we can follow God in love.

VI. Because love on our part must be pleasing to God. Some men think that they please Him chiefly by theological zeal; but how miserably have we got away from the essential things and become occupied with the unessential.

VII. Because hereby we express our love towards God. We express our gratitude to the Source of our redemption.

THREE HUNDRED OUTLINES OF SERMONS
ON THE NEW TESTAMENT
JENNINGS & GRAHAM

* * * * *

CHRIST ALL IN ALL
I am Alpha and Omega (Rev. 1:8).

There is a threefold setting forth of Christ in the New Testament. The conception of the Evangelists embodied in the narrative of the Gospels. The reflected picture seen in the effects produced on the people; they feared, wondered, etc. Christ's own setting forth of Himself in the titles He assumed. Here we have a part of it. The self-presentation of the glorified Christ. He here identifies Himself with God, whose peculiar title is "the first and the last." In many ways is Christ the Alpha and Omega.

I. HE IS ALPHA AND OMEGA OF CREATION.

It began in His thought (Rom. 11:36); was made by His power (John 1:3); exists through His bounty (Heb. 1:3); has its issue in His praise and glory (Col. 1:16).

II. HE IS ALPHA AND OMEGA OF HISTORY.

The years before Him we mark B.C.; the years after A.D. The centuries before were a preparation for His advent. History since has been a record of His triumphs.

III. HE IS ALPHA AND OMEGA OF SCRIPTURE.

He appears in Genesis, "The seed of the woman." He is the grand figure in Revelation. He the subject of all between.

IV. HE IS ALPHA AND OMEGA OF SALVATION.

He is author and finisher of our faith. He convinces and converts. He justifies and sanctifies. There is none other name.

V. HE IS ALPHA AND OMEGA IN THE LIFE OF THE BELIEVER.

He is crucified with Christ. He lives for Christ. To live is Christ—to know, love, glorify, be like, work for, enjoy, Christ. So Paul says, "Whose I am, whom I serve."

VI. HE IS ALPHA AND OMEGA IN THE CHRISTIAN CHURCH.

He is foundation and head corner stone. He began it. He has been with it. He is with it. He shall gather it, and glorify it.

THE PREACHER'S AND TEACHER'S VADE-MECUM
Compiled by J. Ellis
ALLENSON & CO. LIMITED

*   *   *   *   *

THE PERFECTION OF HEAVEN
Rev. 22: 1-5

I.   A RIVER OF WATER OF LIFE—Fruitfulness.

II. NO MORE CURSE—Blessing.

III. THE THRONE OF GOD AND THE LAMB—Government

IV. HIS SERVANTS SERVE HIM—Service.

V. THEY SEE HIS FACE—Communion.

VI. HIS NAME IN THEIR FOREHEADS—Conformity.

VII. THE REIGN FOR EVER—Glory.

FIVE HUNDRED SCRIPTURE OUTLINES
by
John Ritchie
JOHN RITCHIE, PUBLISHER

* * * * *

Section II
ILLUSTRATIONS

"ABANDONED"

In one of our galleries there is a picture of an old derelict vessel, an old battered hulk, on a rough sea with threatening clouds, and forked flashes of lightning shooting across it. It is a picture by Stanfields which he calls "Abandoned." No canvas ever spoke its message with plainer voice. I might describe it. I might comment on it. But down underneath the painting is a verse that tells the whole weird, pathetic story. Listen to the words:

> Storm-beaten, torn and tossed
> By night and day;
> Lone, lorn, lamented, lost,
> Drifting away.

What a picture of many a soul!—*Life and Light.*

* * * * *

ALWAYS NEW

Old John was a man of God and loved his village chapel. One day he was stopped by an acquaintance, who, by the way was an ardent angler. "I say, John," said the angler, "I have often wondered what attraction there is up at the village chapel. You go week after week to the same old chapel, see the same folks, sing the same old hymns—." "Wait a minute," interrupted John. "You fish very often at the same spot, and in the same water, do you not?" "Yes, that's true," agreed the other. John smiled, and then exclaimed: "Well, you do not, for the water you fished in yesterday has passed on to the sea, and every time I go up to the chapel the Lord has something fresh for me."—*Christian Beacon.*

* * * * *

BE YE ALSO READY!

A Christian doctor in London wanted to arouse his pageboy as to the salvation of his soul. One night he explained how "the Lord Himself shall descend from heaven with a shout" (I Thess. 4:16), and concluded, "When the Lord comes, you may have my house, John." The boy looked surprised. "And my carriages"—more surprise; "and my furniture, and money." "Thanks," gasped the boy. Alone in bed he began to think, "If the doctor goes to heaven, what will I do with his house, his carriage, etc.? Where will I be?" He aroused his master, explained his desire, was pointed to Christ, and ere morning was also ready. Do we live as if we really expected the Lord to come at any time? Do others see that expectancy in us and in our manner of life?—*The Philippine Evangelist.*

* * * * *

THE BEST MEDICINE

Dr. Hyslop, one of Britain's greatest physicians, said to the British Medical Association: "The best medicine which my practice has discovered is prayer. As one whose whole life has been concerned with the sufferings of the mind, I would state that of all hygienic measures to counteract disturbed sleep, depression of spirits, and all the miserable sequels of a distressed mind, I would undoubtedly give first place to the simple habit of prayer. It is of the highest importance, merely from a physical point of view, to teach children to hold daily communion with God. Such a habit does more to quiet the spirit and strengthen the soul to overcome mere incidental emotionalism than any other therapeutic agency known to man."

* * * * *

BIBLE—COMFORT OF THE

After the battle before Richmond had been over several days a man was found dead with his hand on the open Bible. The summer insects had taken the flesh from the hand, and there was nothing but the skeleton fingers lay on the open page, and on this passage—"Yea, though I walk through the valley of the shadow of death, I will fear no evil; Thy rod and Thy staff they comfort me." Well, the time will come when all the fine novels we have on our bedroom shelf will not interest us, and all the good histories and all the exquisite essays will do us no good. There will be one Book, perhaps its cover worn out and its leaf yellow with age, under whose flash we shall behold the opening gates of heaven.—*Talmage.*

1001 ILLUSTRATIONS FOR PULPIT AND PLATFORM
by
Rev. Aquilla Webb
Richard R. Smith, Inc.

* * * * *

BIBLE—ENOUGH KNOWLEDGE OF IT TO POISON A PARISH

A little girl being asked by a priest to attend his religious instruction, refused, saying it was against her father's wishes.

The priest said she should obey him, not her father.

"Oh, sir, we are taught in the Bible, 'Honor thy father and thy mother.'"

"You have no business to read the Bible," said the priest.

"But, sir, Our Savior said, 'Search the Scriptures.'"—John 5:39.

"That was only to the Jews, and not to children, and you don't understand it," said the priest in reply.

"But Paul said to Timothy, 'From a child thou hast known the Holy Scriptures.'"—II Tim. 3:15.

"Oh," said the priest, "Timothy was being trained to be a Bishop, and taught by the authorities of the church."

"Oh, no, sir," said the child; "he was taught by his mother and his grandmother."

On this the priest turned her away, saying she "knew enough of the Bible to poison a parish."

SEED CORN FOR THE SOWER
by
Rev. C. Perren
FLEMING H. REVELL

* * * * *

BIBLE—HOW TO DEAL WITH ITS DIFFICULTIES

An old man once said, "For a long period I puzzled myself about the difficulties of Scripture, until at last I came to the resolution that reading the Bible was like eating fish. When I find a difficulty I lay it aside, and call it a bone. Why should I choke on the bone when there is so much nutritious meat for me? Some day, perhaps, I may find that even the bone may afford me nourishment."

FEATHERS FOR ARROWS
by
C. H. Spurgeon
PASSMORE & ALABASTER

* * * * *

BIBLE PRESCRIPTION

The Bible is God's apothecary shop. Here are prescriptions for:

CARE: "Be careful for nothing."

DOUBT (as to doctrine): "If any man will do his will, he shall know of the doctrine," etc.

DOUBT (as to duty): "If any man lack wisdom, let him ask of God."

FEAR: "Perfect love casteth out fear."

GREED: "Seek first the kingdom of God," etc.

PRIDE: "Be clothed with humility."

LUST: "Walk in the Spirit, and ye shall not fulfill the lust of the flesh."

SELFISHNESS: "He that loveth his life shall lose it," etc.

AMBITION: "Seekest thou great things for thyself? Seek them not."

ANGER: "Let all anger be put away from among you."

HEARTACHE: "He bindeth up the broken heart."

—*War Cry*

* * * * *

THE BIBLE

The Bible is so great a Book that nations can read their doom within its covers; it is such a deeply personal Book, that the lowliest heart can find comfort and strength from its pages.—*The Presbyterian.*

* * * * *

THE BIBLE TEST

An exchange tells of a Mohammedan trader in India, who once asked a European whether he could not secure a Bible for him. "What for?" he asked in surprise, "You would not be able to read it."

"True," replied the Mohammedan. "What I want is a European Bible."

When the European asked, "What for?" he answered:

"Well, when a ship brings a trader who is unknown to me who wishes to trade with me, I put the Bible in his way and watch him. If I see that he opens it and reads it, I know that I can trust him. But if he throws it aside with a sneer or even a curse, I will have nothing to do with him, because I know that I cannot trust him."—*Christ Life and Word of the Cross.*

* * * * *

THE BLACK SPOT

A certain man was asked to talk to a company of business men about the depression. He tacked up a big sheet of white paper. Then he made a black spot on the paper with his lead pencil, and asked a man in the front row what he saw. The man replied promptly, "A black spot."

The speaker asked every man the same question and each replied, "A black spot." That was what he had expected. Then with calm and deliberate emphasis the speaker said: "Yes, there is a little black spot but none of you saw the big sheet of white paper. That's my speech."

What do we see? Of course there is a "black spot." But do we see the big sheet of white paper, which represents our opportunities, our blessings, and the challenge of today and tomorrow? Matthew Arnold wrote of Wordsworth that he "saw life steadily and saw it whole." That inspiring phrase expresses wisely and well the comprehensive conception of life which we all need. We see the spots. We see the obstacles, the clouds and the depressions. But do we see enough? Do we see the heights and the lights in God's firmaments?—*The Standard*

* * * * *

BOTH KNEES NEEDED

A lecturer recently declared at the outset of his lecture that he "received his moral training at the knee of a devout mother and across the knee of a determined father." One wonders how many of the on-coming generation will be enabled to make such a statement.

* * * * *

BRINGING THEM IN

A missionary physician in one of China's hospitals cured a man of a cataract. A few weeks later, forty-eight blind men, from one of China's interior provinces, each holding on to a rope held in the hand of the man who had been cured, came to the hospital. Thus in a chain they had walked 250 miles to the doctor, and nearly all were cured.

Does not this incident give a picture of our share in the missionary enterprise? The first blind man came to the physician, put his trust in him, received his sight, and then went out to lead others to him. If your Savior has given you spiritual sight, what have you ever done for missions? What would happen if all did their share?—*The King's Business*

* * * * *

CHILD, INFLUENCE OF A

A Christian mother, who had been attending some of Mr. Moody's meetings (in Dundee, in 1874), taught her little girl, a child scarcely three years of age, to say, "Jesus loves me, even me." Her father, who would not be prevailed on by his wife to go to any of the meetings, on returning from his work one evening was met by the little one at the door, saying, "Pa, Jesus loves me. Jesus loves even oo (you)." Her father's heart was touched, tears filled his eyes. The little one had accomplished what exhortation had failed to do, and he went to hear for himself what was thus commended to him by baby lips.—*The Christian*

FIFTEEN HUNDRED FACTS AND SIMILES
by
J. F. B. Tinling
Funk & Wagnalls Company

* * * * *

CHILDHOOD TRUST

There is no more beautiful sight than a child resting in its father's arms. And that rest means something more than physical rest, which mere sleep might secure. If this were all the child would better rest in its crib, which would be much more comfortable. There is a far deeper meaning in the longing which the child has to creep into its father's arms and go to sleep. Even when the child has been punished, it will at once climb into the father's arms, and with a deep sigh cuddle down to rest. It is spiritual rest which the child craves, and it rests in the father's love more sweetly than in his arms.

Let this child grow up to be a young man just entering life, just beginning to battle with the realities of life; and you will see him now and then returning, weary, disheartened, almost discouraged, to have a good talk with the old gray-haired father in whose arms he lay in infancy, and who has been along the rugged path of life before him.

This father love is not a permanent thing, and we learn by it to look higher, to a heavenly Father who never grows old. Christians may look to God with the same confidence and trust which children have for earthly parents. They may rest in his smile and may fly to his arms even when his chastisements fall.

OLD TRUTHS NEWLY ILLUSTRATED

by

Henry Graham, D. D.

EATON & MAINS

* * * * *

COMPLETE CONSECRATION

Suppose a mother gives her child a beautiful flower-plant in bloom, and tells her to carry it to a sick friend. The child takes the plant away, and when she reaches the friend's door she plucks off one leaf and gives it to her, keeping the plant herself. Then afterwards, once a week, she plucks off another leaf, or a bud, or a flower, and takes it to the friend, still retaining the plant. Has she obeyed? Nothing but the giving of the whole plant would be obedience. Yet, God asks for all our life—heart, soul, mind, and strength; and we pluck off a little leaf of love now and then, or a flower of affection, and give these little things to Him, keeping the life itself. Shall we not say, "Let Him take all"?

* * * * *

A CONFESSION

"Almighty God, as I sit here this lovely Sunday morning surrounded by the paper and half listening to one of the big preachers over the radio, it has just come to me that I have lied to Thee and to myself. I said I was not well enough to go to church. That was not true. I would have gone to the office if it had been Monday morning. I would have played golf if it had been Wednesday afternoon. I would have attended my lunch club if it had met this noon. But it was Sunday morning, and Sunday sickness seems to cover a multitude of sins. God, have mercy on me, I have lied to Thee and myself. I am not sick, I am lazy. Amen."

* * * * *

CONSECRATION

"Will you please tell me in a word," said a Christian woman to a minister, "what your idea of consecration is?" Holding out a blank sheet of paper the pastor replied, "It is to sign your name at the bottom of this blank sheet, and let God fill in as He wills."—*Christian Victory*

* * * * *

A DEAD CHURCH

Someone tells the story of an artist who was once asked to paint a picture of a decaying church. To the astonishment of many, instead of putting on the canvas an old, tottering ruin, the artist painted a stately edifice of modern grandeur.

Within the grand entrance was an offering plate of elaborate design for the offerings of fashionable worshipers. But—and here the artist's idea of a decaying church was made known—right above the offering plate there hung a square box bearing the legend, "For Missions," and right over the slot through which contributions ought to have gone he had painted a huge cobweb.—*Michigan Christian Advocate*

* * * * *

DEAD UNTO SIN

In God's sight we are dead to sin and alive to Him. We should act, when sin tempts us, as though we were literally dead, giving absolutely no response to the temptation.

In a western town several years ago, there lived a young woman who was the main figure in all of the social activities, and a favorite with all. An evangelist came to town, but Lucy repeatedly refused to attend the meetings. However, she finally went on the last night, and was saved. The transformation was complete and marvelous. No longer could she be persuaded to attend the former social gatherings. Instead, she sought the fellowship of Christians. Because the social activities were dead in Lucy's absence, her worldly friends decided on a scheme to get her back. After surprising her on the evening of her birthday, the spokesman of the group declared, "Lucy, we have reserved seats at the theater for tonight, and we want you to accompany us. We are doing this for you, to show how highly we esteem you." Lucy promptly refused saying, "I cannot go, and I am very sorry that you have done this. Really, I have never attended the theater in my life and I would be entirely out of place. No, I cannot go." "Why, Lucy, you know you have attended our theater parties. You were always the very life of them." "Not I," said Lucy, "I buried the girl who went to the theater."—*Moody Monthly*

*   *   *   *   *

DEATH, VIEWS OF

"I am taking a fearful leap in the dark," said the dying infidel Hobbes.

"This is heaven begun. I have done with darkness for ever. Nothing remains but light and joy for ever," said the dying believer, Thomas Scott.—*Family Treasury*

FIFTEEN HUNDRED FACTS AND SIMILES
by
J. F. B. Tinling
FUNK & WAGNALLS COMPANY

*   *   *   *   *

DIED IN HIS PLACE

Dwight L. Moody used to tell the story of the days when the gold fever swept California. A man went West, leaving his wife and son in New England. Soon he succeeded and sent for his loved ones. The wife's heart leaped for joy. Taking her boy to New York, she boarded a Pacific steamer sailing for San Francisco. The ship had not been long out at sea before there was a cry of "Fire! Fire!" On board was a powder magazine and the captain knew that the moment the fire reached the store, all on board would perish. Lifeboats were crowded, but they proved to be too small and few. Quickly they were overcrowded. As the last boat pushed away the mother pled with the boatman to take her and the boy. "No, I dare not take another. If I do, we shall all sink," was the reply. Earnestly the woman continued to plead, and at last the boatman consented to take one. Do you think the mother leaped into the boat, leaving her boy to perish with the others? No, she seized him, gave him one last hug, and dropped him into the boat with the wail, "My boy, if you live to see your father, tell him that I died in your place." And if he did live, do you think he spoke contemptuously of the mother who went down into a watery grave for him?—*Herbert Lockyer*

*   *   *   *   *

DIVINE

One of England's leading actors was being banqueted. In the after-dinner ceremonies the actor was asked to recite for the pleasure of the guests. He consented, and asked if there was anything special anyone in the audience would like to hear.

There was a moment's pause, and then an old clergyman spoke up. "Could you, sir," he said, "recite the twenty-third Psalm?"

A strange look came over the actor's face, but he was speechless for only a moment. "I can, sir—and will, on one condition, and that is that after I have recited, you, my friend, will do the same."

"I?" replied the surprised clergyman; "but I am not an elocutionist. However, if you wish, I will do so"

Impressively the great actor began the Psalm, holding his audience spellbound. As he finished, a great burst of applause broke from the guests.

After the applause had ceased, the old clergyman arose. The audience sat in tense silence. The Psalm was recited, and when it was done, there was not the slightest ripple of applause, but those in the audience whose eyes were yet dry had their heads bowed.

The great actor, with hand on the shoulder of the old clergyman, his voice trembling, exclaimed, "I reached your ears, my friends, but this man reached your hearts; I know the twenty-third Psalm, but this man knows the Shepherd."

* * * * *

DO WE GLORIFY GOD?

One day recently, a lady was crossing a certain London station, when an old man stopped her, and said: "Excuse me, ma'am, but I want to thank you for something." "Thank me!" exclaimed the lady. "Yes'm. I used to be ticket collector at ——, and whenever you used to go by you allays give me a cheerful smile and a 'good mornin',' and you don't know what a difference it made to me. Wet or fine, it was always the same, and I thinks to meself, 'Wonder where she gets her smile from; one cannot be always happy, yet she seems to,' and I know'd that there smile must come from inside somehow. Then one mornin' you comes by and you had a little Bible in yer hand, and I says to meself, 'P'r'aps that's where she gets her smile from.' So as I went home that night I bought a Bible, and I've been readin' it, and I've found Christ, and now I can smile too, and I want to thank yer."—*The Way of Faith*

*   *   *   *   *

DOES CHRIST LIVE HERE?

Bishop Charles L. Slattery tells the following story he heard in a little church in France:

A new pastor had come to the village, and called at a certain cottage. When the husband came home from his work the wife said, "The new pastor called today."

"What did he say?" asked the man.

"Oh," she answered, "he asked, 'Does Christ live here?' and I didn't know what to say."

The man's face flushed: "Why didn't you tell him that we were respectable people," he said.

"Well," she answered, "I might have said that; only that isn't what he asked me."

"Then why," continued the husband, "didn't you tell him that we say our prayers and read our Bibles?"

The wife replied, "But he didn't ask me that."

The man grew more vexed. "Why," he continued, "didn't you say that we were always at church?"

The poor woman broke down; "He didn't ask that either; he asked only, 'Does Christ live here?' "

This man and woman pondered for many days what the grave pastor meant by his question. Little by little their lives were changed; little by little they grew to expect Christ, not dead, but gloriously alive. And some way, they knew not how, through great love, and through a willingness to be surprised by the mystery of His radiance, they knew Him. He did indeed live there!—*The Pilot.*

* * * * *

THE EFFECTUAL FERVENT PRAYER

Dr. Wilbur Chapman wrote to a friend, "I have learned some great lessons concerning prayer. At one of our missions in England the audience was exceedingly small; but I received a note saying that an American missionary . . . was going to pray God's blessing down upon our work. He was known as Praying Hyde. Almost instantly the tide turned. The hall became packed, and at my first invitation fifty men accepted Christ as their Savior. As we were leaving I said, 'Mr. Hyde, I want you to pray for me.' He came to my room, turned the key in the door, and dropped on his knees, and waited five minutes without a single syllable coming from his lips. I could hear my own heart thumping, and his beating. I felt the hot tears running down my face. I knew I was with God. Then, with upturned face, down which the tears were streaming, he said, 'O God!' Then for five minutes at least he was still again; and then, when he knew that he was talking with God . . . there came up from the depths of his heart such petitions for men as I had never heard before. I rose from my knees to know what real prayer was. We believe that prayer is mighty and we believe it as we never did before."

* * * * *

THE ELOQUENT WOUND

History informs us of two brothers, one of whom, for capital crimes, was condemned to die. But on the appearance of the other, who had lost an arm in the defense of his country, there was a stay of sentence; and when he held up the stump of the severed member, the judges were so affected by the recollection of his past service that for his sake they relented, and pardoned the guilty brother.

The Redeemer, presenting himself "as a Lamb that was slain," pleading for his people the merits of his sufferings and death, never pleads in vain.

THE GOSPEL WORKER'S TREASURY
Compiled by Rev. E. S. Lorenz
FLEMING H. REVELL COMPANY

* * * * *

ENLIGHTENED

A Bible was given to Don Gregorio, a Venezuelan, who commenced to read it from its beginning. Before reaching Exodus 12, he learned that he was a member of a ruined, sinful race. In reading this chapter, he thought that what God had demanded then ought still to be of benefit. So, he with the use of a kid, performed the rites of the passover, putting the blood on the door posts of his house, roasting the kid, and eating it with his family. He still continued to read his Bible, and learned through the New Testament that this was but a type of Christ, our Passover slain for us. He believed and was saved.—*Good News*

* * * * *

FAITH—TRIUMPH OF

During an earthquake that occurred a few years since, the inhabitants of a small village were generally very much alarmed, but they were at the same time surprised at the calmness and apparent joy of an old lady whom they all knew. At length one of them, addressing the old lady, said: "Mother, are you not afraid?" "No," said the mother in

Israel; "I rejoice to know that *I have a God that can shake the world.*"

FEATHERS FOR ARROWS
by
C. H. Spurgeon
Passmore & Alabaster

* * * * *

FARADAY'S "SPECULATIONS"?

"I know that my redeemer liveth." When Michael Faraday was dying—and he had the intellect of ten ordinary men—someone said to him, "Mr. Faraday, what are your speculations now?" "Speculations?" said Faraday. "I have none, I thank God. I am not resting on guesswork, I KNOW that my Redeemer liveth, and because He lives, I shall live also."—*Baptist Bulletin.*

* * * * *

FIRST THINGS LAST

When he gets up at four o'clock to deliver papers, they call him a go-getter.

If church work required getting up at four, they would say, "That's expecting far too much."

If she spends eight hours away from home for the cannery or the bean patch, they call her an enterprising housewife.

If she did the same for her church, they'd say, "Religion has gone to her head."

If we tie ourselves down with $30.00 a month for the pleasure of a car, we know we must pay, and we pay.

But if we were to walk instead and pledge the $30.00 to the work of God, people would call us crazy.

This is a crazy world, where first things come last and last things first.—*Southern Witness.*

* * * * *

GEMS—HIDDEN ONES

"What dirty, dreadful, disgusting stuff," exclaims a man regarding that peculiarly unpleasant compound, the mud of London streets. "Hold, my friend," says Ruskin. "Not so dreadful after all. What are the elements of this mud? First there is sand, but when its particles, are crystallized according to the law of its nature, what is nicer than clean white sand? And when that which enters into it is arranged according to a still higher law, we have the matchless opal. What else have we in this mud? Clay. And the materials of clay, when the particles are arranged according to their higher laws, make the brilliant sapphire. What other ingredients enter into the London mud? Soot. And soot in its crystallized perfection forms the diamond. There is but one other—water. And water when distilled according to the higher law of its nature, forms the dewdrop resting in exquisite perfection in the heart of the rose." So in the muddy, lost soul of man is hidden the image of his Creator, and God will do His best to find His opals, His sapphires, His diamonds and dewdrops—*Rainsford.*

SEED CORN FOR THE SOWER
by
Rev. C. Perren
FLEMING H. REVELL

* * * * *

GIVE OR TAKE

The collector approached a parishioner and held out the box.

"I never give to missions," whispered the parishioner.

"Then take something out of the box, sir," whispered the collector; "the money is for the 'eathen."

PUNGENT PARAGRAPHS
Compiled by Leewin B. Williams
LEEWIN B. WILLIAMS AND SON

* * * * *

GIVING

"A man in a New England town had been unemployed so long that he came to his last dollar. He laid fifty cents of it on the offering plate on Sunday. The following morning he heard there was a possibility of his obtaining employment in a neighboring town. The railroad fare to the town was a dollar. It looked as if he should have kept the fifty cents he laid on the offering plate; but with the fifty cents that he had he bought a ticket, and rode half way to his desired destination. He stepped from the train and started to walk to the town. But God had something better for him. Before he had gone a block he learned of a factory near at hand that needed help. Inside of thirty minutes he had a job with a wage of five dollars more a week than he would have received had he gone on to the other town. The first week's pay brought back his fifty cents tenfold. That man was W. L. Douglas, the shoe manufacturer.—*One Besetting Sin* by Charles F. Weigle

* * * * *

GOD HEARS

A friend of mine said to a life-saver at Newport, R. I.: "How can you tell when anyone is in need of help when there are thousands of bathers on the beach and in the water making a perfect hub-bub of noises?" To which he answered: "No matter how great the noise and confusion, there has never been a single time when I could not distinguish the cry of distress above them all. I can always tell it." And that is exactly like God. In the midst of the babel and confusion he never fails to hear the soul that cries out to Him for help amid the breakers and storms of life.

1001 ILLUSTRATIONS FOR PULPIT AND PLATFORM
by
Rev. Aquilla Webb
RICHARD R. SMITH, INC.

* * * * *

GOD IS NOWHERE

"God is nowhere," was the fool's motto which an infidel lawyer nailed up in his office. One day his little daughter spelled out the words, but made a mistake in dividing the letters, "God-is-now-here." Her father corrected her, but she soon read it wrong again. The trifling circumstance impressed the man so much that he finally abandoned his infidelity, and became a worshiper of the ever-present God.

THE GOSPEL WORKER'S TREASURY
Compiled by Rev. E. S. Lorenz
FLEMING H. REVELL COMPANY

* * * * *

GOD IS OMNIPRESENT

One Sunday morning an instructor in a theological school was sharing a seat with a small boy on a shuttle train, states the "Philadelphia Bulletin." The boy was holding a Sunday-school lesson leaflet.

"Do you go to Sunday school, my boy?" asked the man in a friendly way.

"Yes, sir."

"Tell me, my boy," continued the man, thinking to have some fun with the lad, "tell me where God is, and I'll give you an apple."

The boy looked up sharply at the man and promptly replied: "I will give you a whole barrel of apples if you will tell me where He is not."—*War Cry*.

* * * * *

GOING ANOTHER WAY

The Rev. Dr. Witherspoon, formerly president of Princeton College, was one on board a packet ship, where among other passengers, was a professed atheist, who said he did not believe in a God and a future state, not he! By and by there came a terrible storm, and the prospect was that all would go to the bottom. There was much fear and consternation on board, but no one was so horribly frightened as the atheist. In his extremity he sought out the clergyman. He found him and in the cabin, calm and collected, and thus addressed him: "O Mr. Witherspoon! We're all going down; we have but a short time to stay. We're all going down, don't you think we are, Doctor?" Dr. Witherspoon turned on him a look of most provoking coolness, and replied in broad Scotch: "Nae doot, nae doot, mon, we're a' ganging; but you and I dinna gang the same way."—*The Presbyterian*

* * * * *

A GOOD ANSWER

A New Hebrides Chieftain sat peacefully reading the Bible, when he was interrupted by a French trader. "Bah," he said in French, "why are you reading the Bible? I suppose the missionaries have got hold of you, you poor fool. Throw it away! The Bible never did anybody any good."

Replied the chieftain, calmly, "If it wasn't for this Bible, you'd be in my kettle there by now!"—*The Pentecostal Evangel*

* * * * *

GRACE—GROWTH IN

There is a Chinese fable about a man who, in order to make his garden produce faster, went over it and pulled his plants a little further through the ground. He was rejoicing in his foresight only to find that his plants were dead. It takes time to be holy. You can't do it on toadstool principles.

1001 ILLUSTRATIONS FOR PULPIT AND PLATFORM
by
Rev. Aquilla Webb
RICHARD R. SMITH, INC.

* * * * *

THE GREAT COMFORT OF A GOOD CONSCIENCE

A prisoner standing at the bar, in the time of his trial, seemed to smile, when heavy things were laid against him; one that stood by asked him, why he did smile? Oh, said he, it is no matter what the evidence say, so long as the judge says nothing. And to speak truth, it is no matter what the world says, so long as conscience is quiet; no matter how cross the wheels go, so as the clock strikes right; unspeakable is the comfort of a good conscience, unconceivable is the joy, when God and a good conscience smile upon a man in the midst of reproach and trouble, and false imprisonment; for those cannot be scandal where a good conscience speaks fair; that cannot be a prison where a good conscience is the keeper; but that is a sad case, when there are clamors abroad and a noise within, when a man is outwardly smitten with bitter things, and inwardly tormented with a guilty conscience.

CYCLOPEDIA OF BIBLE ILLUSTRATIONS
WORTHINGTON CO., PUBLISHERS

* * * * *

THE GREAT LEVELER

Three people came forward one Lord's day to be received into the membership of a Baptist church in Washington, D.C. One was Charles Evans Hughes, who had come to Washington to be Secretary of State of the United States, and one was a poor working woman, and one was a colored man. The pastor of the church said to the congregation, "You will note that the ground is level at the Cross!" —*Earnest Worker*

* * * * *

GRIEVANCES

If a man is wounded he puts a bandage over the wound and keeps it out of sight till it heals. If he takes the bandage off and shows it to everyone he meets it will never heal. And people do not like to have old sores shown to them. It is a disgusting spectacle. Not more so than to have persons uncover their old grievances and rehearse them to all they meet. Injuries ten, twenty years old are kept fresh and sore by this process, and people are disgusted by the recital of them.

OLD TRUTHS NEWLY ILLUSTRATED
by
Henry Graham, D. D.
EATON & MAINS

* * * * *

HEAVEN

There is much pathos in a little story telling of the meeting of Wilberforce, the great Christian statesman and reformer, and Robert Hall, the eminent English divine. In the course of their conversation Hall said to Wilberforce: "What is your idea of heaven?" To this Wilberforce replied: "Love, Mr. Hall; love, love. And what is yours?"

And Hall answered: "My idea of heaven is rest, rest."
Both men evidently spoke at that moment out of the fulness
of their nature—the large, loving heart of Wilberforce,
which sighed for a larger and more expansive world; and
the poor, wretched, racked body of Hall, which never knew,
for long years, a day's liberation from pain. Heaven will
be the satisfaction of all the soul's needs.

WINDOWS FOR SERMONS
by
Louis Albert Banks
FUNK & WAGNALLS CO.

*   *   *   *   *

HE WAS A "POOR HEATHEN"

A certain rich man did not approve of foreign missions.
One Sunday at church, when the offering was being taken
up, the collector approached the millionaire and held out
the bag. The millionaire shook his head. "I never give to
missions," he whispered. "Then take something out of the
bag, sir," whispered the collector. "The money is for the
heathen."—*The Outlook*

*   *   *   *   *

HOW AFRICANS PREACH THE GOSPEL

It is a well-known characteristic of the African preacher
to illustrate the truth he wants to drive home. A missionary in Kenya sends some examples of the way they make
the truth real and vivid:

"Do you find it very hard work being the only Christian,
perhaps, in your village? You are like a *gitugi* (the forked
stick that props up a bunch of bananas): the owner of the
garden has put you there, and He wants the fruit of all in
your village to be His. If you were not there it might fall

to the ground and be spoilt; so even if it is hard, or you are persecuted, go on witnessing for Christ."

"The native beehive hangs in the tree waiting for the wild bees to swarm into it. Let us become like the beehive, and receive the Lord Jesus as the bee to dwell in it. Then He will bring His own honey, and our lives shall be full of sweetness."

One pastor prayed as follows: "O God, we are Thy cooking pots. Give us the fire and the water that we need, so that the food for Thy children may not be spoiled, and the children go hungry. Thou art the *murugi* (mother who cooks); use us to cook food for Thy children."

And another prayer: "Father, there is a little piece of my garden I have always been ashamed of, and I have never wanted any one to see. Dig your *panga* (cultivating knife) in deep, and cultivate it for me."—*C. M. S. Outlook*

* * * * *

HUMILITY

In a certain church some gossip was started about two aged men, saints of God, who had through many years served in that church. It was whispered about that these two were having a fuss with each other and could not agree between themselves. The gossip, like fire, spread and became more defiling in its accusations.

A wise Christian went to the older of the two men and said, "I am so sorry to learn that you and Brother . . . are not able to get along with each other. It grieves our hearts to hear that you are having such a dispute. Tell me, what is the trouble, so that we may pray about it."

The saint of God replied, "Yes, it is a very serious dispute between my brother and myself. He claims that he is the weakest and worst of the saints in this church and I claim that I am. I really feel that I am way below him in spiritual vision and in usefulness. He will not have it that way and claims he is way below me. I do not know how we shall get this difficulty settled. We shall just continue to pray about it and let our Lord settle it for us."—*The Evangelical Christian*

* * * * *

"I KNOW THAT MY REDEEMER LIVETH"

Reichel was conducting the final rehearsal of his great choir for the production of the "Messiah." The chorus had sung through to the point where the soprano solo takes up the refrain, "I know that my Redeemer liveth." The soloist's technique was perfect—she had faultless breathing, flawless enunciation. After the final note all eyes were fixed on Reichel to catch his look of approval. Instead he silenced the orchestra, walked up to the singer with sorrowful eyes, and said, "My daughter, you do not really know that your Redeemer liveth, do you?" "Why, yes," she answered, flushingly, "I think I do." "Then sing it," cried Reichel. "Tell it to me so that I will know and all who hear you will know that you know the joy and power of it." Then he motioned the orchestra to play again. This time she sang the truth as she knew it and had experienced it in her own soul, and all who heard wept under the spell of it. The old master approached her with tear-dimmed eyes, and said, "You do know, for you have told me."

* * * * *

JESUS STRONGER THAN SATAN
I John 4:4

A little boy came to his father, looking very much in earnest, and asked, "Father, is Satan bigger than I am?"

"Yes, my boy," said the father.

"Is he bigger than you, Father?"

"Yes, my boy, he is bigger than your father."

The boy looked surprised, but thought again, and then asked, "Is he bigger than Jesus?"

"No, my boy," answered the father; "Jesus is bigger than he is."

The little fellow, as he turned away, said with a smile, "Then I am not afraid of him."

"Little children . . . greater is He that is in you, than he that is in the world."

THE GOSPEL WORKER'S TREASURY
Compiled by Rev. E. S. Lorenz
FLEMING H. REVELL COMPANY

*   *   *   *   *

"KEEP ME!"

Once I had an indifferent servant girl, and my wife said to her, "Go home, I don't want you any longer." But the girl stood there and said: "I don't want to go. I know I am the poorest servant you ever had, but keep me." And if Christ should come down today and discharge me, I would fall on my knees and say: "Great Christ, I know I am the poorest servant you ever had, but keep me; oh, keep me!"

SAM JONES ANECDOTES
RHODES & McCLURE PUBLISHING CO.

*   *   *   *   *

KEEP YOURSELF OUT OF SIGHT

Seeking diversion by fishing in the streams of Scotland, a literary man went from the city with patent pole and a complete outfit of the most expensive kind. After hours of effort without even a bite, he came across a country boy with only a switch for a pole and a bent pin for a hook—but he had a long string of fish.

"Why is it that I can't catch any?" the man inquired.

"Because you don't keep yourself out of sight," the boy replied.

This is the secret of fishing for men as well as trout. Hold up the cross of Christ. Send the people away talking about Him, instead of praising you.—*The Volunteer*

*   *   *   *   *

THE LANGUAGE OF LOVE

The language of love is not getting, but giving. Mr. Robert E. Spear relates a beautiful incident illustrative of the love for Christ and mankind, a love that finds its true expression in self-sacrifice. A missionary family was returning, after a rest in America, to the work in Tabriz, Persia. As the little party came to the crest of the hills that shut the great plains of Tabriz off from the Aras River and Mt. Ararat and Russia to the north, its members stopped to look across the gray plain, to the gray city and the great red rocky hills beyond, which gather up the sun and fling it down like javelins into the city. It was a dreary sight after the green fields of home, and one of the little girls at last looked up into her mother's face, and said: "It's not nearly so nice as America, mother, is it?" "No, my child," the mother replied; "that's why we've come." There was love in those hearts, and so there was loving service in those lives. That is love's way of showing itself, and of being love.

WINDOWS FOR SERMONS
by
Louis Albert Banks
FUNK & WAGNALLS CO.

*   *   *   *   *

LET GOD RULE

Oliver Cromwell's secretary was dispatched to the continent on some important business. He stayed one night at a seaport town, and tossed on his bed, unable to sleep.

According to an old custom, a servant slept in his room, and on this occasion slept soundly enough. The secretary at length awakened the man, who asked how it was that his master could not rest.

"I am so afraid something will go wrong with the embassage," was the reply.

"Master," said the valet, "may I ask a question or two?"

"To be sure."

"Did God rule the world before we were born?"

"Most assuredly He did."

"And will He rule it again after we are dead?"

"Certainly He will."

"Then, master, why not let Him rule the present, too?"

The secretary's faith was stirred, peace was the result, and in a few minutes both he and his servant were in sound sleep.—*Gleanings*

* * * * *

THE LIFE

This story is told of a Christian teacher in a government school in the Orient. He was employed with the understanding that during school hours he should not utter a word on the subject of Christianity. This contract was faithfully kept. He lived before his students the Christ life, but never was a word spoken to them about Jesus. So blameless was his example, so spotless was his character, so Christlike was his spirit shown before these students that

without his knowledge forty of the students met in a grove
and signed a covenant to abandon idolatry."

* * * * *

LIKE THE SILLY OX

A man whose sin had brought shame and disgrace upon
him, and who is trying to fight his way back again to respect
by divine help, uttered these words of warning the other
day: "Let me raise the red flag of warning that others may
escape my sad experience. Strong drink and evil companions brought me to ruin. How easily it was done! You
have seen the butcher pat the neck of the silly ox until he
had him noosed for slaughter! So was I led by flattering
plaudits till locked and bolted behind prison bars." That
is a graphic description, written as it were, in a man's life-
blood. It recalls the words of the Scripture that there is a
way which seems right to a man, but the end of that way
is death.

ANECDOTES AND MORALS
by
Rev. Louis Albert Banks
Funk & Wagnalls Company

* * * * *

LITTLE SINS

The following was told in the address of a converted
Burman to a group of natives.

A little banyan seed said to a palm tree, "I am weary of
being tossed about by the wind; let me stay a while among
your leaves."

"Oh, yes," said the palm tree, "stay as long as you like,"
and by and by forgot the little seed was there. But the
seed was not idle. It sent out little fibers and tiny roots,
and they crept around the trunk and under the bark and

into the heart of the tree itself. Then the tree cried out, "What is this?"

The banyan said, "It is only the little seed you allowed to rest among your leaves."

"Leave me now," said the palm tree. "You have grown too large and strong."

"I cannot leave you now; we have grown together. I will kill you if I tear myself away."

The palm tree bowed its head and tried to shake the banyan off, but could not, and little by little the palm tree withered, the trunk shriveled, and only the banyan could be found.

Beware of little sins!—*The Pilot*

* * * * *

LIVING TO DIE

A writer in the Church Union tells this story: The writer's grandfather had an old negro workman who had been a slave, and was used to the severest kind of labor. No need of a slave-driver for him, however, as his tasks were conscientiously performed. "Corporal," as the old slave was called, was of a religious turn, and believed with an unalterable firmness in the truths brought to him. Finally the time came for "Corporal" to leave this world. The doctor said to him: "Corporal, it is only right to tell you that you must die." "Bless you, Doctor; don't let that bother you: that's what I've been living for," said Corporal, with the happiest of smiles.—*Christian Beacon*

* * * * *

LOOKING ON THE WRONG SIDE

Dr. G. F. Pentecost was once trying to comfort a woman who had passed through sore trials. Failing in his efforts to cheer her and dispel her doubts, he took up some embroidery upon which she had been working and said, "What a confusion of threads! Why waste time on a thing like that?" Turning the embroidery over, she said, "Now look at it. You were seeing it from the wrong side." "That's it, exactly," said Dr. Pentecost. "You are looking at your trials from the wrong side. Turn them over and look at them from the right side—that is, from God's side. The Lord is working out a design of His own for your life, and you must look at things from His point of view, and trust His workmanship."—*Edwin M. Kerlin*

* * * * *

THE LONG DAY OF JOSHUA

This is perhaps the most frequently used argument which is directed against the authority of the Bible.

Professor Totten of Yale includes the following story in one of his books:

A fellow-professor who was an accomplished astronomer, made the strange discovery that the earth was twenty-four hours out of schedule. Professor Totten challenged this astronomer to begin at the beginning of the Bible and read as far as need be to see if the Bible could account for the missing time.

Upon coming to the account of the long day of Joshua, the skeptical astronomer rechecked his figures and found at the time of Joshua there were only twenty-three hours and twenty minutes lost. This was enough to convince the man that the Bible was not the Word of God, because here was a mistake of forty minutes. However, Professor Totten pointed out that the Bible does not say twenty-four hours, rather "about the space of a whole day."

Reading further, the astronomer found in Isaiah the thrilling story of King Hezekiah, who was sick unto death.

God, in answer to the king's prayer, had promised to add fifteen years to his life. To confirm the truth, God sent Hezekiah out to his court to watch the shadow of his sundial turn back ten degrees. Ten degrees on the sundial is forty minutes on the face of a clock.

When the astronomer found his day of missing time thus accounted for, he laid down the book and worshipped its Writer, saying, "Lord I believe."—*From Gary B. Y. P. U. Paper.*

* * * * *

LOYALTY TO CHRIST

After Mr. Gladstone had been married fifty years he said one day to a friend, "My wife has known every political secret I have ever had and has never betrayed my confidence." On one occasion in Mr. Gladstone's early days of cabinet office his young wife dropped a word in the presence of some of his colleagues which implied that she knew some matter of confidential importance. Immediately realizing that she had made a slip, she left the room and wrote a penitential note, which she sent in by a servant. Instantaneously came back the reply: "Dearest C—. Don't blame yourself. I don't blame you. It is the only little mistake you ever made. Your affectionate W. E. G." Paul uses the ideal relation between husband and wife as an illustration of the relation that should exist between the Christian and Christ. Every one of us should be as loyal to Jesus as Mrs. Gladstone was to her husband, and we may be sure that if we are He will be still more gentle with us than the great Prime Minister was to the wife to whom he was so devoted.

WINDOWS FOR SERMONS
by
Louis Albert Banks
Funk & Wagnalls Co.

* * * * *

LYING TO GOD

The minister's little daughter was never forgetful of her formal prayers, and had been allowed the privilege of adding any original remarks that she saw fit. One night in the late fall, at the close of her prayer she added: "And, dear Lord, please send the beautiful snow to keep the little flowers warm through the winter."

Climbing into bed, she confided: "That's the time I fooled Him. I want the snow so I can go sliding with my new sled!"

That girl isn't the only one who lies to God in prayer. May we have a personal heart-searching, and ask God to deliver us from all efforts to lie to Him in prayer. Charles Finney once told a church they could not have a revival until the elders stopped lying to God in prayer.—*Christian Victory.*

* * * * *

MEETING THE AUTHORS

Many years ago Dr. Bonar was speaking on heaven and the great reunion of loved ones over there, and in his eloquent way he pictured the believer newly come from the earth walking along the golden street and suddenly coming right up against a group of Old Testament sages and prophets. In a moment he recognizes them and says, "Why, this is Ezekiel, isn't it?"

"Yes," says Ezekiel, "I am so glad to meet you."

"And this is Micah and Zechariah and Amos."

And then Andrew Bonar said, "And just imagine Ezekiel saying, 'Oh, you knew about me, did you? How did you like the book I wrote?'

"Book? What book was that? I am sorry to say I never read it.

"And then Micah would say, 'And what did you think of my book?'

" 'Let me see, was that in the Old Testament or in the New Testament? It seems to me I remember there was such a book.'

"How would you feel to have to meet these men and never have read their books?"

Some of you better get busy. There is far too much time spent in reading novels and in reading the newspapers and too little time given to the Word of God. Good literature is fine; reading the newspaper is all right, but these things should not crowd out time for reading God's Word.—*The Moody Church News*

* * * * *

MIRACLES OF THE DUST

Professor E. Slosson of Washington, an analytical chemist of high reputation, declares that the amazing accuracy of verbal detail which distinguishes the Bible, even in chemistry, has driven him to render homage to the "Book of books" as the "Word of God." The second chapter of Genesis states that God formed man of the "dust of the ground." Prof. Slosson assures that these simple words are charged with the deepest scientific meaning. He says that "the dust of the ground" contains just fourteen out of the ninety-two chemical elements known to science, and that the flesh of man is composed of precisely the same fourteen elements. English scientists also confirm this interesting statement as a recognized fact of chemical science.— *Gospel Herald.*

* * * * *

MISSIONS AND OMISSIONS

Life without a mission is life with a tremendous omission. To leave off life's mission would be like leaving off the flanges of the engine's wheels or the rudder of the ship. Direction would be lost. Mate Frank Bullen tells us, in his sea stories, that a cruel sport is to catch a shark, and after cutting off its ventral fins, to return it to the water. It has no longer any power to direct its course, all its convulsive efforts merely send it shooting wildly to the surface. Even so do we treat our lives who would destroy the purpose, the mission, in them. Those who tell us we can do nothing and are going nowhere are both false and cruel. The divine voice tells us that there is a baptism to be baptized with, and that we are straitened until it is accomplished. Nothing is more deadly to a true life than omission of its mission.— *Sunday School Times*

* * * * *

THE MODERNIST AND THE FUNDAMENTALIST

Walter Lippman, the newspaper man, in concluding his imaginary dialogue between a Modernist and a Fundamentalist, makes the Modernist ask that the question be discussed without heat. But the Fundamentalist says, "Has it ever occurred to you that this advice is easier for you to follow than for me?" "How so?" asks the Modernist. "Because for me an eternal plan of salvation is at stake. For you there is nothing at stake but a few tentative opinions, none of which means anything to your happiness. Your request that I should be tolerant and amiable is, therefore, a suggestion that I submit the foundation of my life to the destructive efforts of your skepticism, your indifference, and your good nature. You ask me to smile and to commit suicide."—*Gospel Message*.

* * * * *

G. CAMPBELL MORGAN'S CALL TO FAITHFULNESS

In one of his earlier pastorates, we are told, G. Campbell

Morgan had an impressive experience. At the close of a Sunday evening message, as he sat alone in his study, the question came to him as clearly as though spoken by some one in the next room:

"What are you going to be, a preacher or My messenger?"

He went back over the evening sermon and was convinced that he was wanting to be known as a great preacher. For hours he sat pondering that question and praying. Finally he gave his answer: "Thy messenger, my Lord. If Thou wilt give me Thy words to speak, I will utter them, from this day forward, adding nothing to them, taking naught away."

* * * * *

"MOTHER, I LOVE YOU"

A pleasant-faced woman boarded a trolley car with her two small sons during the busy noon hour of the holiday season. The smaller boy sat with his mother on one side of the car while the other, who was about four years old, took a seat opposite. It interested him to look out of the window, but frequently he glanced across at his mother. At length he called softly, "Mother!" No answer. Again he spoke: "Mother!" This time it was said a bit louder, and the mother looked over and smiled.

The boy's eyes lighted, and he whispered: "Mother! I love you." The mother turned a glorified face upon her small son, and men and women in the car looked tenderly from one to the other. The trolley car had suddenly become a place of blessing because a little boy had voiced this ever-beautiful sentiment: "Mother, I love you."—*The Defender*

* * * * *

MUCH ZEAL

An Indian having heard from a white man some strictures on zeal, replied, "I don't know about having *too much zeal*, but I think it is better the pot should boil over, than not boil at all."

INSTRUCTIVE ANECDOTES ILLUSTRATIVE OF
THE OLD AND NEW TESTAMENTS
by
John Whitecross
SIMPKIN, MARSHALL, HAMILTON, KENT & CO.

*   *   *   *   *

"MY MOTHER'S BEEN PRAYING"

In February, 1861, a terrible gale raged along the coast of England. In the Bay Hartlepoole it wrecked eighty-one vessels. While the storm was at its height, the Rising Sun, a stout brig, struck on Longrear Rock, a reef extending a mile from one side of the bay. She sank, leaving only her two topmasts above the dashing and foaming waves.

The life-boats were away rescuing wrecked crews. The only means of saving the men clinging to the swaying masts was the rocket apparatus. Before it could be adjusted, one mast fell. Just as the rocket bearing the life-line went booming out of the mortar, the other mast toppled over.

Sadly the rocket-men began to draw in their line, when suddenly they felt that something was attached to it, and in a few minutes hauled onto the beach the apparently lifeless body of a sailor-boy. Trained and tender hands worked, and in a short time he became conscious.

With amazement he gazed around on the crowd of kind, sympathizing friends. He looked up into the weather-beaten face of the old fisherman near him and asked:

"Where am I?"

"Thou art safe, my lad."

"Where's the cap'n?"

"Drowned, my lad."

"The mate, then?"

"He's drowned, too."

"The crew?"

"They are all lost, my lad; thou art the only one saved."

The boy stood overwhelmed for a few moments; then he raised both his hands and cried in a loud voice, "My mother's been praying for me!" and then he dropped on his knees on the wet sand, and put his sobbing face in his hands.

THE GOSPEL WORKER'S TREASURY
Compiled by Rev. E. S. Lorenz
FLEMING H. REVELL COMPANY

* * * * *

NO TIME FOR EFFICIENCY

How short-sighted many people are in not taking time for the strengthening of their spiritual life, is illustrated by this little gem from *Now:*

"A sweating wood chopper who wasn't doing well was urged to stop and sharpen his ax. He snorted: 'It's tough enough now getting this job done without taking time out to grind an ax.'"

* * * * *

NOT WASTED

A young woman, who was a great lover of flowers, had set out a rare vine at the base of a stone wall. It grew vigorously, but it did not bloom. Day after day she cultivated it and watered it, and tried in every way to coax it into bloom. One morning, as she stood disappointedly before it, her invalid neighbor, whose back lot adjoined her own, called over and said: "You can't imagine how much I have been enjoying the blooms of that vine you planted." The owner looked, and on the other side of the wall was a mass of blooms. The vine had crept through the crevices and flowered luxuriantly on the other side.

There is a lesson for every Christian here. So often we think our efforts thrown away because we do not see their fruit. We need to learn that in God's service our prayers, our toil, our crosses are never in vain. Somewhere they bear their fruit and some hearts will receive their blessing and joy.—*Forward*

* * * * *

"O GOD, FOR A BIGGER BOAT"

The many tragedies at sea, caused by the present war, and the heroic effort put forth to save the lives in each instance, calls to mind the disaster of the Princess Alice which collided with another boat in a dense fog on the river Thames half a century ago. The boat was crowded with excursionists and the loss of human lives was great, about 600 perishing in the dark waters. Mr. Herbert Lockyer tells of an interesting little sidelight of the tragedy concerning two ferrymen, which is worth repeating.

It appears that these two ferrymen were mooring their boats for the night close at hand, when the crash happened. One heard the crash and the cries, and said, "I am tired and I am going home; no one will see me in the fog." At the coroner's inquest, both had to appear. The first was asked:

"Did you hear the cries?"

"Yes, sir."

"What did you do?"

"Nothing, sir."

"Are you an Englishman? Aren't you ashamed?"

"Sir, the shame will never leave me till I die."

Of the other the coroner asked:

"What did you do?"

"I jumped into my boat and pulled for the wreck with all my might; I crammed my boat with women and children, and when it was too dangerous to take even one other, I rowed away with the cry, 'O God, for a bigger boat!'"

There are thousands of men and women shipwrecked in the waters of sin, lost and doomed to an eternal death and punishment in hell. The Christian who has been gripped by this fact, and who is earnestly trying to save some out of the many, may well cry: "O God, for a bigger boat." The apostle Paul was having a feeling something like that when he cried: "I could wish that myself were accursed from Christ for my brethren," for they were lost without Christ.—*Brethren Missionary Herald*

* * * * *

PARDON, NOT JUSTICE

In the days when Napoleon was the first consul of France, a well-dressed girl of fourteen years of age presented herself alone at the gate of the palace. By tears and entreaties she moved the kind-hearted porter to allow her to enter. Passing from one room to another, she found her way to the hall through which Napoleon with his officers, was to pass. When he appeared, she cast herself at his feet, and in the most piteous and moving manner cried: "Pardon, sir! pardon for my father!"

"And who is your father?" asked Napoleon, "and who are you?"

"My name is Layolia," she said, and with flowing tears added, "but, sir, my father is doomed to die."

"Ah, young lady," replied Napoleon, "I can do nothing for you. It is the second time in which your father has been found guilty of treason against the State."

"Alas!" exclaimed the poor girl, "I know it, sire, but *I do not ask for justice—I implore pardon!* I beseech you, forgive, oh, forgive my father!"

Napoleon's lips trembled, and his eyes filled with tears. After a momentary struggle of feeling he gently took the hand of the young maiden, and said: "Well, my child, for your sake I will pardon your father. That is enough. Now leave me."

Reader, whoever you are, know that as a sinner against God, the cry from your lips must also be: "Not justice, but pardon!"

> SEED CORN FOR THE SOWER
> by
> Rev. C. Perren
> FLEMING H. REVELL

* * * * *

PENALTY OF SUCCESS

A remarkable instance of the penalty of success is reported by persons living near Jamestown, N. Y. For many years a colony of American eagles had made its home near the shores of Chautauqua Lake. They had not been molested and had grown bolder in their depredations.

Not long since one of them was noticed hovering over the lake, and its graceful flight was watched by several persons. Suddenly it darted with lightning rapidity toward the water, catching in its talons a muskellunge two feet or more in length, and weighing probably ten pounds. There was a clash and splashing of fins and feathers, but slowly the bird rose in the air with its captive dangling and wriggling below. When at a height of about 1,000 feet the bird, still clinging to the fish, began to sink slowly toward the lake again gaining speed as it descended, and finally fell with a splash in the water. Later, the bird and fish were found together dead.

The eagle had evidently found the fish too heavy to carry, but had been unable to drop it, owing to its claws being so firmly imbedded in the flesh that it could not release its hold, and as its strength gave way it sank into the water whence it had sought its prey and was drowned. The very tenacity with which the eagle grasped its prize prevented its losing it when it wished to do so.

It is often so with men who discover when too late that some eagerly coveted prize is proving fatal to them.—*Watchword and Truth.*

* * * * *

A PERFECT STANDARD

Experts in London, after ten years of patient work, have finished the most perfect yardstick in the world. It is made of platinum and iridium and was designed to be used as the standard of the British Government. Every fourteen years it will be examined, and if it varies by a millionth of an inch, it will be rejected.

The Bible never varies by the shadow of a hair. It is the perfect standard for righteous living. "The law of the Lord is perfect" (Ps. 19:7).

PICKINGS
by
Robert G. Lee
ZONDERVAN PUBLISHING HOUSE

* * * * *

A PLEASANT PARABLE

Little Willie was asked if he ever studied the Bible.

"Yes, sir," he replied.

"Then, of course you know all about the parables," said the questioner.

"Yes, sir," said Willie.

"Good!" replied the questioner. "And will you tell me which parable you like best?"

"I like the one where everybody loafs and fishes," said Willie.—*New York Evening Post*

PUNGENT PARAGRAPHS
Compiled by
Leewin B. Williams
LEEWIN B. WILLIAMS AND SON

* * * * *

THE POLISHED BOOTS

Dr. Stuart Holden in *The Sunday at Home* tells the following incident on soul winning. When on a visit in Egypt, in one of his meetings among soldiers, Dr. Holden asked a big sergeant in a highland regiment how he was brought to Christ. He said, "There was a private in the same company who was converted in Malta before the regiment came to Egypt. We gave that fellow an awful time. One terrible wet night he came in very tired and very wet. Before getting into bed he got down to pray. My boots were heavy with wet mud, and I let him have one on one side of the head, and the other on the other side; and he just went on with his prayers. Next morning I found those boots beautifully polished and standing by the side of my bed. That was his reply to me and it broke my heart. I was saved that day."—*Alliance Weekly*

* * * * *

THE POWER OF GOD'S WORD

It is said that once when the late C. H. Spurgeon was to preach in the great Crystal Palace in London, he went there one morning to test his voice in the building. Mounting the platform he uttered these words, "This is a faithful saying, and worthy of all acceptation, that Christ Jesus came into the world to save sinners."

Twenty-five years later Spurgeon's brother was called to see a dying man who told this story. "Twenty-five years ago I was working one morning on the dome at the Crystal Palace. I was a rank unbeliever. Suddenly there came a voice saying, 'This is a faithful saying, and worthy of all acceptation, that Christ Jesus came into the world to save sinners.' That day I gave my heart to Christ, and have served Him ever since."—*Winnipeg Bible Institute Bulletin*

* * * * *

PRAYER PLUS

The Watchman-Examiner recalls that upon one of D. L. Moody's journeys across the Atlantic there was a fire in the hold of the ship. The crew and some volunteers stood in line to pass buckets of water.

A friend said to Moody, "Mr. Moody, let us go to the other end of the ship, and engage in prayer."

The common-sense evangelist replied, "Not so, sir; we will stand right here and pass buckets and pray hard all the time we are doing so."

How like Moody this was! He believed that prayer and work were like the two hands of the one person, in that they should never be separated.

* * * * *

PRAYER REACTION

Prayer pulls the rope below and the great bell rings above in the ears of God. Some scarcely stir the bell for they pray so languidly; others give an occasional pluck at the rope; but he who wins with heaven is the man who grabs

the rope boldly and pulls continually with all his might.—
C. H. Spurgeon

* * * * *

"PRAY WITHOUT CEASING"

A friend once asked General "Stonewall" Jackson, says a writer in "Revelation," what was his understanding of the Bible command to "Pray without ceasing." "I can give you my idea of it by illustration," he answered, "if you will allow it and not think I am setting myself up as a model for others. I have so fixed the habit in my own mind that I never raise a glass of water to my lips without lifting my heart to God in thanks and prayer for the water of life. Then, when we take our meals, there is grace. Whenever I drop a letter in the post office, I send a petition along with it for God's blessing upon its mission and the person to whom it is sent. When I go to my classroom and await the arrangement of the cadets in their places, that is my time to intercede with God for them. And so in every act of the day I have made the practice habitual."—*Pentecostal Evangel*

* * * * *

PRAYING FORBIDDEN

An officer once complained to Stonewall Jackson that some soldiers were making a noise in their tent.

"What are they doing?" asked the general.

"They are praying now, but they have been singing," was the reply.

"And is that a crime?" the general demanded.

"The article of war orders punishment for any unusual noise," was the reply.

"God forbid that praying should be an unusual noise in this camp," replied General Jackson.—*Selected*

* * * * *

PROCRASTINATION

What if a man going to San Francisco should make preparations for his journey from Brooklyn to Hoboken, and no further. Would you not call him a fool? But here he postpones his preparation until the very last moment of time. The distance from here to the grave is smaller when compared with eternity, than the distance from here to Hoboken is small compared with the thousands of miles between here and San Francisco. Here is a man who thinks only of the three or four yards of human life, and regards not the millions of furlongs stretching out into the infinite.

GEMS OF TRUTH AND BEAUTY
by
Rev. Charles C. Albertson
RHODES & McCLURE PUBLISHING CO.

* * * * *

PROVIDENCE MYSTERIOUS

Alpine guides often blindfold the traveler who seeks to ascend to those awful heights where dwell eternal frost and ice. When the danger is past, the bandage is removed, and the traveler sees for the first time the slippery path along which he has been led.

In like manner our Heavenly Father mercifully conceals the future with its trials and dangers till we are safely past. All that He hides is hidden in mercy; and all that He reveals is revealed in love. I would not know all, my Father. It is known to Thee, and that is enough. "We walk by Faith, and not by Sight." "Blessed are they who have not seen and have believed."

SEED CORN FOR THE SOWER
by
Rev. C. Perren
FLEMING H. REVELL

* * * * *

PURITY OF CONVERSATION

It is related that General Grant was once sitting in his tent with officers around him, when a general came in in much glee and said:

"I have a good story to tell; there are no ladies present, I believe."

"No," said General Grant, "but there are *gentlemen* present."

The man's countenance fell; the good story was never told. Some Christians could learn a good lesson from the great commander's remark.—*Christian (Boston)*

FIFTEEN HUNDRED FACTS AND SIMILES
by
J. F. B. Tinling
FUNK & WAGNALLS COMPANY

* * * * *

RECIPE FOR CHARM

A dear old Quaker lady, distinguished for her youthful appearance, was asked what she used to preserve her charms. She replied sweetly: "I use for the lips, truth; for the voice, prayer; for the eyes, pity; for the hands, charity; for the figure, uprightness; and for the heart, love."
—Jerry Fleishmann *Moody Monthly*

* * * * *

RESIGNATION

Several gentlemen visited a school in France, in which was a boy who was both deaf and dumb. One of the gentlemen asked him, who made the world? The boy took his slate and wrote the first verse of the Bible, "In the beginning God created the heaven and the earth." He was then asked, "How do you hope to be saved?" The child wrote, "This is a faithful saying, and worthy of all acceptation, that Christ Jesus came into the world to save sinners." The last question proposed was,—"How is it that God has made *you* deaf and dumb, while all those around you can hear and speak?" The poor boy seemed puzzled for a moment, and a suggestion of unbelief seemed to pass through his mind, but quickly recovering himself, he wrote, "Even so, Father, for so it seemed good in Thy sight."

INSTRUCTIVE ANECDOTES ILLUSTRATIVE OF
THE OLD AND NEW TESTAMENTS
by
John Whitecross
SIMPKIN, MARSHALL, HAMILTON, KENT & CO.

* * * * *

THE RESTFUL YOKE

Mark Guy Pearse tells us of an incident which occurred in connection with a sermon of his on Christ's invitation to the weary and heavy-laden:

"I had finished my sermon, when a good man came to me and said: 'wish I had known what you were going to preach about. I could have told you something.'

" 'Well, because the good Lord helps us to carry it, I suppose.'

" 'No, sir,' he exclaimed, shaking his head; 'I think I know better than that. You see, when I was a boy at home, I used to drive the oxen in my father's yoke. And the yoke was never made to balance, sir, as you said.' (I had referred to the Greek word. But how much better it was to know the real thing.)

"He went on triumphantly: 'Father's yokes were always made heavier on one side than the other. Then, you see, we would put a weak bullock in alongside a strong bullock, and the light end would come on the weak bullock, because the stronger one had the heavy part of it on his shoulder.'

"Then his face lit up as he said: 'That is why the yoke is easy and the burden is light—because the Lord's yoke is made after the same pattern, and the heavy end is upon His shoulder.'

"So shall ye find rest to your soul."—*Gospel Herald*

* * * * *

RESULTS OBTAINED ONLY TEMPORARILY

The mother of some colored children, says The Sunday School Times, was disturbed by a racket in her kitchen. Going to the kitchen, she discovered that her little black baby boy was wallowing in the flour barrel.

"Land sake, sonny," she said, "What am de matter wid you?"

She listened to his tale of woe. He didn't like the white boys calling him "Nigger," so he was going to be like white boys! His old mother roared with laughter, and said to him, "My boy, you'll never be white, even though you use all the flour in that barrel. You is black 'cause it's in your blood. But listen, sonny boy, what is more important, de Lord He done shed His blood at Calvary that you and me might have hearts washed white. Better have a black skin and a white heart, dan a white skin and a black heart. Dat flour can only white-wash you, but Jesus' blood can wash you white!"

* * * * *

REVIVAL CONVERSIONS

I have more faith (put this down in your memorandum-book), I have more faith in men who are brought to God during revivals than during a frigid state of the church. I have had close observation in these things. Stand two men side by side. Let them have equal endowments. You tell me that this man was brought in when the church was very cold, and the other was brought in while the church was very warm in revivals. I will say, "Give me the last one; I had rather have him than five of the other kind."

When are we going to get the world converted? When the people in solid columns march into the Kingdom of God, not by ones, but by tens, fifties and hundreds. Oh, that the Lord would upturn this church with holy revivals! Oh, that such days might come as Richard Baxter saw in Kidderminster, as Jonathan Edwards saw in Northampton, as McCheyne saw in Dundee! "O, Lord, revive thy work!"

GEMS OF TRUTH AND BEAUTY
by
Rev. Charles C. Albertson
RHODES & McCLURE PUBLISHING Co.

* * * * *

THE RICE OF LIFE

The following story came direct to us from Rev. Mr. Cunningham of South China:

One day a well-dressed, intelligent-looking man came to the Street Chapel. He sat and listened well for some time, then left. This was repeated three consecutive days. Then he rose and addressed the Missionary, saying—

"I have heard you speak three times and you always have the same text. Why don't you change it?" Mr. Cunningham somewhat surprised asked "What text?" "Jesus Christ" was the reply. After a moment's silence the missionary replied—

"Sir, before answering your question, may I ask you: What had you for dinner today?"

"Rice," replied the man.

"What food had you yesterday?" Again came—

"Rice."

"And what do you expect to eat in the future," the missionary asked.

"Rice, of course. Rice gives me strength. I could not do without it. Sir: It is—he hesitated as if for a strong enough word—Sir: It is my very life."

The missionary raised his hand, "That is just what I wanted from you. What you have said of rice, Jesus Christ is to our souls. He is the Rice of Life."—(*Mrs. J.*) *Rosalind Goforth*

* * * * *

ROBBING GOD

A Chinese preacher, speaking of robbing God, used this illustration: "It came to pass that a man went to market with a string of seven coins. Seeing a beggar that asked for alms, he gave the poor man six of the coins and kept one for himself. The beggar, instead of being thankful, followed the good man and stole the seventh coin also. What an abominable wretch! Yes, and would you, to whom God has given six days, steal the seventh also?"—*The Presbyterian*

* * * * *

SACRIFICE

Alexander Duff spent most of his long career in India. At the end of his life he came to Edinburgh and spoke at a great convention. For two and a half hours he held the audience spellbound as he told about the trials and hardships and about the conquests in the mission field. At the end of that period he fainted, and they carried him off the platform. When his consciousness was restored, he cried out: "Take me back, I must finish my message." His attendants protested and said: "You will die if you go back." "I'll die if I don't," was his answer.

Again he stood before that magnificent audience and poured out his heart. "Have you no more sons to send to India? Queen Victoria asks for soldiers and you gladly offer your sons. Christ asks for missionaries, and you say, 'No, we have no sons to send.' If there is no one who will volunteer, I'll go back to India, and let them know that there is one Scotchman that is willing to die for those who sit in heathen darkness."

Shall we not be inspired by the example of Alexander Duff to obey the call of God and go to the ends of the earth for our wonderful Christ? He died for us, shall we not live for Him and, if needs be, die for Him?—*Paul W. Rood*

* * * * *

SAINTS IN WRONG PLACES

I.   ELIJAH—discouraged under a juniper tree (I Kings 17).

II. JONAH—sleeping when men were perishing (Jonah 1).

III. YOUNG PROPHET—deceived because he was disobedient (I Kings 13).

IV. LOT—an ineffective witness because of wrong conduct (Gen. 19).

V.   DAVID—a lazy saint, falls into the Devil's trap (II Sam. 11).

VI. PETER—catches nothing when he fishes without Christ (John 21).

VII. ABRAHAM—backslides, and tells a lie in Egypt (Gen. 12).

—*J. Brown, in The Believer's Magazine*

* * * * *

SAINTS SHOULD GROW IN GRACE

Let the lily be exposed to the scorching sun, and deprived of the refreshing dew, and its leaves will droop and die. Just so the Christian: let him be exposed to the scorching heat of indwelling corruption, the world's cares, and Satan's wiles, without the dew of God's grace, he will not advance in holiness of heart and life. But when that descends, his leaves stand erect, and, like the lily, his growth is rapid. Integrity strengthens, benevolence expands, holiness opens in all its lily-like loveliness, and in due time the plant is removed to the paradise of God, there to bloom in unfading beauty.—*Jackson.*

CYCLOPEDIA OF BIBLE ILLUSTRATIONS
WORTHINGTON CO., PUBLISHERS

* * * * *

THE SHAM ROCK

A street preacher in London was preaching to a crowd that had gathered around him. It was at the time of the Shamrock races, and everyone was talking of the event. A ruffian on the edge of the crowd thought he would have a little fun, so he called three times, "Mr. Preacher! What do you know about the Shamrock?" Finally, the fourth time, not to be silenced, the ruffian called again, "Mr. Preacher! I'm asking you what you know about the Shamrock?" This time the preacher paused. The crowd became very still. Pointing upward with one hand, he said, so clearly and distinctly that every one could hear him, "On Christ, the solid Rock, I stand; all other rocks are—sham rocks!"—*Life and Light*

* * * * *

SIN—POISON OF

A lady caught a little creature which she thought was a chameleon, and attached it by a little chain to her collar, so that it could crawl about on her shoulder. The chameleon is a harmless little reptile, which changes its color from gray to green or red, and is considered very beautiful by some people. Instead of a chameleon, however, this lady caught a poisonous kind of lizard, and it bit her, causing her death. What a terrible mistake! And yet there are many who are taking the poison of sin into their lives, thinking it is a beautiful, pleasant thing. But some day they may find that they have taken something worse than poison into their lives.

1001 ILLUSTRATIONS FOR PULPIT AND PLATFORM
by
Rev. Aquilla Webb
RICHARD R. SMITH, INC.

* * * * *

SOMEONE ELSE IS WATCHING

"Ye shall be witnesses unto me." A friend of mine, who had been a hold-up man and a kidnapper for twelve years, met Jesus Christ in prison. Christ said, "I will come and live in you and we will serve this sentence together," and they did. Several years later he was discharged, and just before he went out he was handed a two-page letter written by another prisoner. After the salutation, it said in effect, "You know perfectly well that when I came into this jail I despised preachers, the Bible, and everything. I went to the Bible class and the preaching service because there wasn't anything else interesting to do. Then they told me you were saved, and I said, 'There's another fellow taking the Gospel road to get a parole'; but, Roy, I've been watching you for two and a half years. You did not know it, but I watched you when you were in the yard exercising, when you were working in the shop, when you played, while we were all together at meals, on the way to our cells, and all over, and now I'm a Christian, too, because I watched you. The Savior who saved you has saved me. You never made a slip." Roy said to me, "When I got that letter and read it through I came out in a cold sweat. Think what it would have meant if I had slipped, even once."—*The Sunday School Times*

* * * * *

SOUL-WINNING BY LOVE

A Christian woman went to the tract house in New York and asked for tracts for distribution. The first day she was out on her Christian errand she saw a policeman taking an intoxicated woman to the station house. After the woman was discharged from custody, this Christian tract distributor saw her coming away all unkempt and unlovely. The tract distributor went up, threw her arms about her neck and kissed her. The woman said, "O my God, why do you kiss me?" "Well," replied the other, "I think Jesus told me to." "Oh no," the woman said, "don't you kiss me; it breaks my heart: nobody has kissed me since my mother died." But that loving, sisterly kiss brought her to Christ, started her on her way to heaven.

GEMS OF TRUTH AND BEAUTY
by
Rev. Charles C. Albertson
RHODES & McCLURE PUBLISHING CO.

* * * * *

SPURGEON AND THE BIBLE

After preaching the gospel for forty years, and after printing the sermons I have preached more than six and thirty years, reaching now to the number of 22,000, in weekly succession, I am fairly entitled to speak about the fulness and the richness of the Bible as a preacher's book. Brethren, it is inexhaustible. No question about freshness will arise if we keep close to the text of the sacred volume. There can be no difficulty about finding themes totally distinct from those we have handled before; the variety is as infinite as the fulness. A long life will only suffice to skirt the shores of this great continent of light. In the forty years of my ministry I have only touched the hem of the garment of divine truth; but what virtue has flowed out of it! The Word is like its Author—infinite, immeasurable, without end. If you were ordained to be a preacher through eternity, you would have before you a theme equal to everlasting demands.—*C. H. Spurgeon*

* * * * *

STAINED WITH HUMAN BLOOD

Dr. George W. Truett tells of a funeral he was asked to conduct of a sixteen-year-old girl. Seeking information that would help him in his ministry of comfort, the mother told him, "Dr. Truett, she was our only child." "Yes, but you sorrow not as others that have no hope," said the minister. The mother answered, "That is where the trouble is, we have no such hope. Our daughter was not a Christian."

The mother wept bitterly while she continued, "While it is true that her father and I were both members of the church even before she was born, it is also true that our darling girl lying in that casket never heard either of us pray. She was not converted, and we fear that she is lost and her blood will be upon us." Then she became hysterical in the thought of a lost daughter.

Relating the incident later, Dr. Truett asked, "Who would dare say that her blood would not be upon them?" Father and mother both professing Christians, but had never prayed in their home! May God have mercy on children coming from such homes!—*The Elim Evangel*

* * * * *

STRENGTH FROM GOD

A man is just as strong as the thing he commits himself to. If I venture out upon the broad ocean in a paper box, as soon as the water has penetrated the box it goes to pieces and I am lost. But if I commit myself to a steamer, neither the storms nor the waves can injure me. If a man commits himself to the flesh, he will be weak as the flesh; but if he commits himself to God he will stand until God goes down. Perhaps you will be afraid to start; you will be mighty weak, but only say, "My hope is in God." Some one will tell you, "You will be tempted all along the way; ten thousand trials will beset your pathway"; but let your answer be, "My hope is in God." Are you weak? Are you tempted? Reach your hand up and take hold of the hand of God. He will strengthen you all along the way. Oh, for a breeze from God tonight that will waft many a soul into the haven of rest!

SAM JONES ANECDOTES
RHODES & McCLURE PUBLISHING CO.

* * * * *

A TEST OF SINCERITY

An old Scotch woman said to her pastor, "That was a grand sermon you preached last Sabbath at the Kirk!"

Seeking to test her sincerity he asked, "And what was the text?"

"Ah, meenister!" she replied. "I dinna ken the text or the words. But I came home and took the false bottom out o' my peck measure."—*The Southern Churchman*

* * * * *

TESTIMONY—LOST

A man who had a sweet singing canary felt that it was a great pity, when spring came, to keep the poor bird in the house, so he decided to hang the cage under a large tree in the yard, for the summer. The tree was the home of many English sparrows, and before he realized what was taking place the little canary had lost all of its sweet notes. It had spent the summer in bad company, and its sweet song never came back. When it was taken in the house in the fall he heard only its monotonous twitter, twitter, twitter. There are some professing Christians who had a beautiful testimony several years ago, but who have lost their witness, and now when they would "speak with the tongues of men and of angels," they "become as sounding brass or a tinkling cymbal." They have broken step with God and lost their experience. My prayer is that we may all learn to walk with Him in the path of Christian fellowship.—*O. A. Newlin*

1001 ILLUSTRATIONS FOR PULPIT AND PLATFORM
by
Rev. Aquilla Webb
Richard R. Smith, Inc.

*   *   *   *   *

THANKSGIVING WITH PRAYER

A child knelt at the accustomed time to thank God for the mercies of the day, and pray for His care through the coming night. Then as usual came the "God bless mother and ——" But the prayer was stilled, the little hands unclasped, and a look of sadness and wonder met the mother's eye, as the words of helpless sorrow came from the lips of the kneeling child, "I cannot pray for father any more."

Since her little lips had been able to form the dear name, she had prayed for a blessing upon it. It had followed close after her mother's name. But now he was dead. I waited for some moments, and then urged her to go on. Her pleading eyes met mine, and with a voice that faltered, she said: "Oh, mother, I cannot leave him all out; let me say, 'Thank God that I had a dear father once'; so I can still go on and keep him in my prayers." And so she still continues to do, and my heart learned a lesson from the loving ingenuity of my child. Remember to thank God for mercies past as well as to ask blessings for the future.—*The Christian*

FIFTEEN HUNDRED FACTS AND SIMILES
by
J. F. B. Tinling
FUNK & WAGNALLS COMPANY

* * * * *

THINGS THAT NEVER HAPPEN IN CHURCH

Ushers calling for help in carrying the offering. Minister insisting that the people attend only one service each Sunday in order to make room for others. A dozen people asking the minister for some really definite work to do during the week. A dozen families asking the ushers to place them on the front seats. Every one in the audience reaching for a hymn-book when the number is announced and then singing heartily. Every head reverently bowed during prayer. No whispering or reading of papers during the service. A choir that does not find a single thing to whisper about during the service. The minister saying, "I have rushed from one thing to another all week. I have spent less than three hours in revising this old sermon which is rather out of date, but I will endeavor to make it fit the occasion." The Ladies' Aid Society hoping that the preacher's wife will bring to the next meeting a long list of things that ought to be done in the parsonage at once. The "old-timers" graciously giving way to newcomers, confident that the newcomers will be able to do much better work than they have done. No one getting up or moving about or leaving the room during the service. The middle pews filled first. Each one speaking to the person next to him at the close of the service and inviting him to come again. The names and addresses of all strangers handed to the minister at the close of the service.—*Brethren Missionary Herald*

* * * * *

"THOU ART THE FINGER"

The story is related of an old deacon who was leading in prayer in a prayer meeting. One of his stereotyped phrases was this, "O Lord, touch the unsaved with Thy finger." As he intoned this phrase in this particular prayer, he stopped short. Other members came to his side and asked if he were ill. "No," he replied, "but something seemed to say to me, 'Thou art the finger.'"—*Otterbein Teacher*

* * * * *

TIDES OF ETERNITY RISING

A gentleman wandering along on the beach of Scotland, where the high rocks came near the sea, was unmindful of the fact that the tide was rising, which would cut off his retreat. A man on the top of the rocks shouted, "Hallo! the tide is rising, and this is the last place through which you can make your escape; you had better climb up on to the rocks." The man laughed at the warning and went on. After awhile he thought it was time to return; he came back and found retreat cut off. He tried to scale the rocks; he clambered half way up—could get no further. The waves came to his feet, came to his waist, came to his chin, and with a wild shriek for help he perished. Oh, brother, the tides of eternity are rising. Those only will be saved who get on the Rock of Ages.—*Talmage*

GEMS OF TRUTH AND BEAUTY
by
Rev. Charles C. Albertson
RHODES & McCLURE PUBLISHING CO.

* * * * *

"TRACKS"

A minister gave a negro a tract. Later, he asked him what he thought of it. "Ah, Massa, it done my soul good. I never knew befo' why dey call dem tracks; but I read dat little book, it track me dis way, and it track me dat way. When I go out in de barn, it tracks me dere; when I come in de house, it tracks me dere; it tracks me eberywhere I go. Den I know why dey call 'em tracks."

* * * * *

THE TRAGEDY OF LITTLE SINS

A mountain eagle, near Gunnison, Colorado, which had been feasting on rabbits, recently met its match. Ferrets had been brought into the valley to kill rabbits. The eagle swooped down upon a ferret. The ferret caught the eagle by the throat and the bird flew far into the air. Only a few minutes elapsed till the eagle came tumbling down. The ranchman who had watched the mid-air battle ran to the fallen bird and found it dead. The ferret had bitten through its throat and was still clinging to it. Many a man has taken some secret sin to his bosom, thinking it so small and easily hidden that there would be no danger; but the sin, like the ferret, has sharp teeth, and to cherish it means certain disaster.

WINDOWS FOR SERMONS
by
Louis Albert Banks
FUNK & WAGNALLS CO.

*   *   *   *   *

UNION—POWER OF

Over the iron bridge that spans the Ohio river are these words, "All military and funeral processions when crossing this bridge must break step." The gigantic structure could not bear the strain of the united muscular movement of a large body of men. In like manner, there is a tremendous moral power in the united efforts of God's people; but alas, they too often break step. What a moral power the church of Christ is in the world, but how much greater its power would be if it was not so divided. Brethren, let us clasp hands and keep step.

SEED CORN FOR THE SOWER
by
Rev. C. Perren
FLEMING H. REVELL

*   *   *   *   *

THE UNREASON OF ENVY

No sin is more silly than envy. The envious spirit often leads its poor victim into the most egregious folly. One day in New York City a sound, well-built man actually bemoaned that fate had not made him a cripple. He stood near Fourteenth Street and Sixth Avenue, trying to sell lead pencils with rubbers attached. He called out lustily, but few people cared to buy. Before him passed a cripple on crutches, who hobbled briskly in and out among the crowd, doing a rushing business in popular song-sheets. As the pencil-vender eyed him in envy, he was heard to mutter, as he stood shivering there, "I wish I had only one leg."

ANECDOTES AND MORALS
by
Rev. Louis Albert Banks
FUNK & WAGNALLS COMPANY

* * * * *

THE VALUE OF A CHILD

Robert B. Pattison gives us the following—as to the value of a child:

A youth is worth $6.50 chemically. He is water and carbon and oxygen and a few other chemical elements.

To his parents his little finger is worth tons of diamonds.

He costs the nation one thousand dollars if he matures righteously and at least another thousand if he does not.

Christ thought enough of him to die for him.

The church weighs him in the scales of eternity. The church opens its doors for him so that jail doors may be tightly closed against him. Juvenile crime decreases when church attendance increases.

What value, then, do you place on every child you see?

PICKINGS
by
Robert G. Lee
ZONDERVAN PUBLISHING HOUSE

* * * * *

A VITAL TRUTH ILLUSTRATED

Evangelist Henry Morehouse once said: "I find a difficulty in the hearts of many in taking their place as guilty sinners before God. Some time ago a woman said to me, 'I cannot see that one who has broken one of the Commandments can be as bad as another who has broken five, or another who has broken the whole ten.' But I told her that God never gave five or ten laws; He gave only one, which consists of ten commandments.

" 'Just look at that watch. If you counted the wheels you would find perhaps ten or more, yet it is a broken watch, and will not go. Yet if you break only one wheel, it is still a broken watch and will not go.' Still the woman could not see it, so I said: 'Suppose you were hanging by a chain over a precipice. The chain consists of ten links. If a man took a hammer and smashed every link, where would you go?' To the bottom, of course.' 'But suppose only one link were broken, where would you go?' 'That would be just as bad; I would fall.'

"It takes just as much grace to save the best people in the world as to save the vilest. Nothing but grace through faith in Jesus Christ can give liberty and freedom from the law of sin."—*Life and Light*

* * * * *

WALKING IN THE LIGHT

A woman in Palestine sat under an olive tree sewing handmade lace upon a handkerchief. A lady paused to inquire the price of her work, and to have conversation. "Do you live here?"

"No, I live over the hill, and last night as I walked home, a panther followed me, but because I carried a lantern and walked in the circle of light, I was safe."

"You mean the panther would not attack you while you were in the light?"

"That is right, madam."

What a lesson for Christians is this!—*The Conqueror*

* * * * *

WASHING THE WOOL

A clergyman walking near a brook, observed a woman washing wool in a stream. This was done by putting it in a sieve, and then dipping the sieve in the water repeatedly, until the wool became white and clean.

He asked the woman if she knew him.

"Oh, yes, sir," she said; "I shall have reason to bless God to eternity for having heard you preach some years ago. Your sermon was the means of doing me much good."

"I rejoice to hear it. Pray, what was the subject?"

"Ah, sir, I can't recollect that, my memory is so bad."

"How then can the sermon have done you so much good, if you don't remember even what it was about?"

"Sir, my mind is like this sieve: the sieve does not hold the water, but as the water runs through, it cleanses the wool; so my memory does not retain the words I hear, but as they pass through my heart, by God's grace they cleanse it. Now I no longer love sin, and every day I entreat my Savior to wash me in His own Blood, and to cleanse me from all pollution."—*Gospel Herald*

* * * * *

WE DO NOT APPRECIATE IT

If a prince, passing by an execution, should take the malefactor's chains, and suffer in his stead, the deed would ring through all history, and be quoted as an amazing instance of heroic pity; and well deserved would be all the words of praise and sonnets of admiration which would record and eulogize it. Yet, our Lord Jesus did this, and infinitely more for those who were not merely malefactors but enemies to His own throne and person. This is a wonder of wonders! But it meets with small praise. The most of men around us have heard of it, and treated it as of little import; as an idle tale; as a pious legend; as a venerable fable; as an unpractical myth. Even those who know, believe, and admire, are cold in their emotions with regard to the story of the atonement. Herein is love which ought to set our hearts on fire, and yet we scarcely maintain a smoldering spark of enthusiasm. Lord Jesus, be more real to our apprehensions, and more completely the master of our affections.—*Spurgeon.*

GEMS OF TRUTH AND BEAUTY
by
Rev. Charles C. Albertson
RHODES & McCLURE PUBLISHING CO.

* * * * *

WHAT A DIFFERENCE!

The difference between listening to a radio sermon and going to church, says an esteemed contemporary is the same as the difference between calling your girl on the telephone and spending an evening with her.

* * * * *

WHY HE DID NOT SEE THEM

"I've been in India for many a year, and I never saw a native Christian the whole time." So spake a colonel on board a steamer going to Bombay. Some days after, the same colonel was telling of his hunting experiences, and said that thirty tigers had fallen to his rifle.

"Did I understand you to say thirty, colonel?" asked a missionary at the table.

"Yes, sir, thirty," replied the officer.

"Because," pursued the missionary, explanatorily, "I thought perhaps you meant three."

"No, sir, thirty"—this time with emphasis.

"Well, now, that's strange," said the missionary; "I have been in India twenty-five years, and I never saw a wild, live tiger all the while."

"Very likely not, sir," said the colonel; "but that's because you didn't know where to look for them."

"Perhaps it was so," admitted the missionary, after a moment or two of apparent reflection; "but may not that be the reason you never saw a native convert, as you affirmed the other evening at this table?"

THE GOSPEL WORKER'S TREASURY
Compiled by Rev. E. S. Lorenz
FLEMING H. REVELL COMPANY

* * * * *

WRONG ORDERS

Some years ago a passenger train was flying into New York as another train was emerging. There was a head-on collision. Fifty lives were snuffed out. An engineer was pinned under his engine. The blood was pouring from his nostrils and tears were running down his cheeks. In his dying agonies he held a piece of yellow paper crushed in his hand, and he said, "Take this. This will show you that someone gave me the wrong orders." Unregenerate men and women will stand before the Great White Throne and point to their modernist preachers saying, "Someone gave me the wrong orders."

* * * * *